FIXIN' TO DIE
RAG

FIXIN' TO DIE RAG

Gooood Morning Vietnam…

We've Just Had a Mid-Air Collision

Roy Mark

Roy Mark
P.O. Box 294
Chiang Mai, 50000
Thailand

Roy@RoyMark.Org
www.facebook.com/Roy.Mark.Books

www.RoyMark.Org

Printed by CreateSpace
Available from Amazon.com and other retail outlets

ISBN-13: 978-1484135105
ISBN-10: 1484135105

SOME GAVE ALL

William Lorimer, IV	16 Jul 1942 – 10 Mar 1970
James Franklin Lee	20 May 1943 – 3 Apr 1970
Ronald Neal Parsons	22 Dec 1948 – 3 Apr 1970
Richard Farley Heath	20 Nov 1947 – 13 Apr 1970
Arnold Lee Robbins	15 Nov 1938 – 15 May 1970
John Richard Stinn	12 Aug 1949 – 15 May 1970
Melvin Ray Thomas	14 Nov 1948 – 15 May 1970
Vernon Gail Bergquist	9 May 1949 – 11 Jun 1970
James Grady Bulloch	5 Feb 1938 – 11 Jun 1970
John Adrian Dossett, Jr.	15 Feb 1951 – 11 Jun 1970
Alonzo Hughes Taylor	9 May 1949 – 11 Jun 1970
Franklin Delano Meyer	1 Dec 1951 – 11 Jun 1970
Raymond Riede Uhl	8 Oct 1948 – 11 Jun 1970
Leslie Miles Tatarski	26 Jun 1948 – 12 Jun 1970
Robert Ernest Bauer	10 Mar 1947 – 26 Sep 1970
Donald Allen Hall, Jr.	13 Jul 1949 – 26 Sep 1970
Mark Richard Holtom	26 Mar 1949 – 26 Sep 1970
Ernest Hammond Laidler	1 Apr 1950 – 26 Sep 1970
Warren Stephen Lawson	22 Oct 1947 – 26 Sep 1970
Robert Albert Painter, Jr.	1 Nov 1949 – 26 Sep 1970
Francis Jordan Sullivan	4 Nov 1942 – 26 Sep 1970
Douglas Mead Woodland	6 Sep 1951 – 26 Sep 1970

Not for fame or reward
Not for place or for rank
Not lured by ambition
Or goaded by necessity
But in simple
Obedience to duty
As they understood it
These men suffered all
Sacrificed all
Dared all-and died

—Reverend Randolph Harrison McKim

CONTENTS

The title of this book and all chapter names are taken from Vietnam War era song titles. Although most of the songs are generally associated with the war, some of the titles may not be immediately recognizable. Readers are encouraged to search the titles on the Internet where numerous copies and versions of the songs are available for listening on video sharing websites.

ABOUT THE COVER

The artwork for the cover of *Fixin' To Die Rag* is taken from a painting by renowned aviation artist Joe Kline. Mr. Kline's original painting, which he titled *Kicking the Hornets Nest*, was an adaptation of a 1969 photo taken in Vietnam by a First Cavalry Division combat photographer. Two years later, the photo appeared on the cover of *Rotor&Wing* magazine. By chance, Roger Baker noticed the cover photograph as helicopters from Charlie Company, 229th Assault Helicopter Battalion, First Cavalry Division. Mr. Baker is a former commander of Charlie Company and recognized immediately that the Hueys in the photograph were from his former unit. Baker and other veterans of Charlie Company studied the photograph and determined that the only pilot recognizable was the right-seat pilot of the lead Huey. That pilot was their commanding officer, Captain William Lorimer, IV. Captain Lorimer was killed by enemy fire a few months later, and his story is told in Chapter Two of this book. Years later, Mr. Kline painted *Kicking the Hornets Nest* based on that photograph.

When I began discussing possible cover designs for this book with Roger Baker, he suggested using *Kicking the Hornets Nest* since it had such significance to the stories told within the book. Mr. Baker contacted Mr. Kline, who graciously granted his permission to use his artwork for the cover. Going beyond simply granting permission, Mr. Kline modified his original painting especially for this book by painting the 229th Assault Helicopter Battalion Crest on the nose of the Hueys in *Kicking the Hornets Nest*.

Joe Kline is a Vietnam Veteran and an Artist Member of the American Society of Aviation Artists.

Joe Kline
6420 Hastings Place, Gilroy, CA 95020
408-842-6979
klinejd569@aol.com

www.joeklineart.com

FOREWORD

The author of this book, Roy Mark, has asked me to write a foreword. As a former Commander of C Company, 229th Assault Helicopter Battalion, First Cavalry Division, I am honored by his request. It is difficult to put into words the profound emotions that have been stirred in researching our story. Forty-four years have passed since we closed that chapter of our lives, and while, in many ways, most of us have tried to put it behind us and move on with our lives, we are still intensely proud of what we accomplished. This book is a great tribute to those of our company who did not return, and a unique legacy for those of us who did return to pass on to our children and grandchildren. Although he never served with us, Roy's literary efforts have earned him an honorable mention in our history.

Roger C. Baker, Major, U.S. Army, Retired

PREFACE

I began writing *Fixin' To Die Rag* as a short story of a mid-air collision of two U.S. Army helicopters during the Vietnam War. Through my research, I met some of the men with first-hand knowledge of the accident, and those veterans began telling me of other tragic events in which good men died. They urged me to include those stories as well. Each event required more research, which in turn introduced me to more of the men that survived their tours in Vietnam. What began as a short story evolved into this book.

Charlie Company of 229th Assault Helicopter Battalion has a long history. This book covers just the period between March and September 1970. During those seven months, Charlie Company lost eighteen of their own. Four soldiers from other companies were lost while flying as passengers with Charlie Company. Twenty-two good men did not live to board that "freedom bird" back to "the world."

Most of the veterans I interviewed told me that it was time their story was told. Some told me that they had suppressed their Vietnam memories for years and have just recently begun to talk about their experiences. One pilot told me that he would not, that he could not, read my book; it would be just too painful. Yet, he encouraged me to continue with my writing; he wanted his story told so that others might begin to understand. I found myself saying, "I understand," but as a non-combat veteran, I feel I can never truly understand.

Roy Mark
October 2014

CONCERNING QR CODES

Most of the photographs reproduced in this book date back to 1969 or 1970. Although most were taken in color, by necessity they appear in this book in black-and-white. In an effort to allow readers the opportunity to view the photos in their original quality, and when applicable in color, I have posted each photo on my website. Below each photo in this book, you will see a QR code similar to the one below.

www.RoyMark.Org

A QR code is a machine-readable optical barcode with stored data. The data in the QR codes that appear below each photo contain the URL web address where the corresponding photo appears on my website.

With the proper app, any smart device such as a smart phone or a tablet computer can scan QR codes. Upon scanning, the smart device will read the URL and automatically open the webpage containing the corresponding photo.

Scanning QR codes with a smart device requires a QR code scanning app. Numerous free scanning apps (or readers) can be downloaded for any smart phone or tablet.

Below the QR codes in this book, I have included the URL for that photo.

ACKNOWLEDGEMENTS

The men of the U.S. Army's First Cavalry Division and particularly Charlie Company of the 229th Assault Helicopter Battalion (C/229th) wrote this book in 1970; I was simply honored to put it into words and bring it to publication some forty-four years later. It was they who lived and died in that terrible war that deserve our gratitude for their sacrifices.

Many people helped create this book, without whom this story could not have been told.

Many of the men you will read about in this book contributed their memories—some very painful—and always, they said, because they thought their stories needed to be told. To each and every one, I am grateful beyond measure.

I am particularly indebted to Daniel E. Tyler, for it was he who wrote a story about a mid-air collision of two C/229th helicopters that caught my attention, and subsequently sparked my desire to begin this journey. Mr. Tyler encouraged me along the way and shared not only his knowledge of certain events but also contact information for many of his fellow C/229th veterans.

One of Mr. Tyler's contacts was Roger C. Baker, who was Tyler's commanding officer in 1970. Mr. Baker became involved with this project, and he, too, was very encouraging and helpful each step along the path to publication.

Many 229th veterans contributed their memories, including Steve Adams, Reg Baldwin, Rod Barber, Robert Barnaba, Neil Blume, Lach Brown, Marvin Collier, Dennis Greek, Larry Heale, David Holte, Robert "Jake" Jacobs, Jack McCormick, Carlton McKoy, Robert Morrow, Mark Panageotes, Robert "Pete" Peatross, John "PJ" Pecha, Steve Reed, Dr. Craig Thomas, Don "Thumpy" Thompson, and Larry Wall.

Special thanks are due Major General Scott Smith and WO1 Neil Blume for their help in telling the story in chapter three. Larry Wall is deserving of our gratitude for sharing his memories of the events surrounding Les Tatarski's death. Thanks too to Gary Roush, webmaster of Vietnam Helicopter Pilots Association website vhpa.org; the information contained on the website was invaluable.

Family and friends of some of the men that sacrificed their lives were kind enough to supply some background information. My gratitude goes to Thaddeus Bara, Christopher Holtom, Gregory Holtom, Michelle Oakley, Sarah Oebser, Andrew Painter, John Riesz, Vikki Shaw, Andrew A. Uhl, and Madonna (Murphy) Wallace.

John Hubbs—a veteran of Charlie and Bravo Companies of 229th—deserves special credit for his assistance and for his creation and maintenance of the 229th website (www.229thavbn.com). His website is a great resource.

Special credit is due C. Douglas Sterner, who is the curator of Military Times Hall of Valor (www.militarytimes.com/hallofvalor) for assistance in verifying certain military medals. My thanks are extended to Cathy Wiemer of Saint John's University in Collegeville, Minnesota and Dana Owen of Lamar High School, Lamar, Missouri for background information on certain of their graduates.

I undoubtedly forgot to mention someone who assisted with this project and to them I sincerely apologize; my memory and record keeping becomes more deficient as the years pass.

—Roy Mark

1 FORTUNATE SON

During the Vietnam War, all gave some, and some gave all. Vietnam was a strange and dangerous place for the young warriors called to service by conscience or country.

Over two and a half million Americans served in uniform during that terrible war, and at least as many stories can be told. Far too many war stories that must be told and remembered are tragic. This book tells but a few of these stories.

Back in "the world", as the troops in Vietnam referred to Stateside, three soldiers were finishing helicopter flight training and awaiting their orders. They were destined to join the 229th Assault Helicopter Battalion of the Army's 1st Cavalry Division. They would fly the UH-1H Iroquois—the "Huey" of Vietnam fame—as co-pilots.

The Iroquois' origin dated back ten years, when in 1960 Bell Helicopters introduced the "Helicopter, Utility" or "HU-1," from whence the nickname "Huey" was derived. In 1963, after taking delivery of the HU-1, the Army changed the designation from HU-1 to UH-1, but the "Huey" tag stuck. Even after the Army officially named the new addition the "Iroquois" (after the American Indian tribe), the name "Huey" would not be denied, and a legend was born.

Bob Bauer, Mark Holtom,[1] and Larry Wall, their new wings shiny upon their chests and warrant officer[2] (WO1) bars upon their collars, were ready for action in Vietnam. Wall arrived at Saigon's Tan Son Nhut Air Base on 28 March 1970 followed by Holtom on 30 March and Bauer on 12 April.

The three new Huey pilots would learn that co-pilots were called "peter-pilots", and upon their arrival in the warzone they would become "FNGs," the Nam abbreviation for "Fucking New Guys."

Apprehension, anticipation, and a dose of culture shock undoubtedly gripped the new arrivals as they traversed the routine of in-country processing. The seemingly never-ending process could drag on for as long as two weeks.

During the days of navigating the Army's in-country processing, the new arrivals' bodies were slowly adapting to the tropical climate of Saigon. Soldiers arriving in South Vietnam in April were greeted with the

---

[1] Mark Richard Holtom (1949 – 1970) was the 4th Cousin of the author.

[2] Warrant officers are highly specialized experts in their career fields. By gaining progressive levels of expertise and leadership, these leaders provide valuable guidance to commanders and organizations in their specialty. Warrant officers remain single-specialty officers with career tracks that progress within their field, unlike their commissioned officer counterparts who focus on increased levels of command and staff duty positions.

country's dry season heat, which averaged 95 degrees Fahrenheit in the afternoons and 80 degrees at night. Bodies did eventually adapt—somewhat.

During processing, Bauer, Holtom, and Wall were given orders to report to the 229th Assault Helicopter Battalion. The 229's base was eighteen miles from the Cambodian border in Tay Ninh Province. Part of the Army's famous 1st Cavalry Division, the 229th was nicknamed the "Stacked Deck Battalion". Their mission was to provide direct support to the 1st Cavalry's 1st and 3rd Brigades.

The 229th Assault Helicopter Battalion was formed in March of 1964 as part of the 1st Cavalry Division at Fort Benning, Georgia. Seventeen months later, on 7 August 1965, the U.S. Congress passed Public Law 88-408, commonly known as "The Gulf of Tonkin Resolution." The resolution authorized President Lyndon Johnson to use military force to resist North Vietnamese aggression. The President wasted little time; orders were issued and preparations began. On 11 September, just 35 days after President Johnson received Congressional approval, the 229th Assault Helicopter Battalion arrived in the Republic of Vietnam.

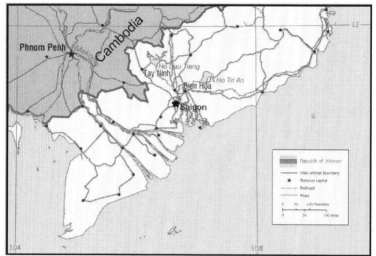

WO1 Bob Bauer, WO1 Mark Holtom, and WO1 Larry Wall reported for duty to the Commanding Officer, 229th Avn. Bn. at Tay Ninh, near the Cambodian border.

www.roy-mark.com/Pics_Fixin/Vietnam_Map.jpg

229th Aviation Battalion Crest
The wing alludes to the flight, the arrowhead to accuracy, the flash to swiftness, and the sword to combat.
With permission of Paul Jensen, Director of Army Trademark Licensing Program

www.roy-mark.com/Pics_Fixin/229-Crest.jpg

229th Assault Helicopter Battalion Patch
Photo Courtesy SP4 John Hubbs
C and B / 229th Avn Bn '71-'72
www.229thavbn.com

www.roy-mark.com/Pics_Fixin/229-Patch.jpg

By 1970, the Stacked Deck Battalion had established itself as a fighting force. The soldiers who had brought the battalion to Vietnam five years earlier were long gone. Many soldiers had come and gone; a few had come and died.

During their short flight from Saigon to their new home in Tay Ninh, Bauer, Holtom, and Wall got their first good view of the Vietnam countryside. The small villages with thatched roofed huts, dirt roads, and rice fields were quite different from their homes half a world away.

Upon their arrival in Tay Ninh, they were assigned to Charlie Company. All companies in the Army were given individual radio call signs, and in the case of Charlie Company, this call sign was "North Flag." It meant nothing to the new guys at the time, but they would soon begin to feel the *esprit de corps* of a very tight, close-knit group of fighting men. Bauer, Holtom, and Wall were now "North Flaggers."

Charlie Company Headquarters at Tay Ninh
North Flag was Charlie Company's' Radio Call Sign
The Company Motto was painted on Damaged Rotor Blades
Photo Compliments of Roger C. Baker

www.roy-mark.com/Pics_Fixin/North_Flag_Name.jpg

Charlie Company, 229th Assault Helicopter Battalion Base at Tay Ninh
Photo courtesy of CWO2 Carlton McKoy
Photo © 2009 Carlton McKoy, All rights reserved
www.cbmckoy.net

www.roy-mark.com/Pics_Fixin/C-229-Tay_Ninh.jpg

2 HELLO VIETNAM

It was a war in transition that the three new warrant officers were thrust into in early 1970. They had just arrived, but many more troops had just departed. By early 1970, the number of troops in Vietnam had been reduced by some 60,000.

The first American military advisers arrived in South Vietnam in 1959, when President Eisenhower sent 760 advisors to help prevent a Communist takeover. The number of advisors increased during the Kennedy years to about 23,000. In 1964, President Johnson began introducing regular ground troops; their numbers soon soared to over 536,000. Richard Nixon's inauguration in 1969 brought about a change in strategy. His "Vietnamization" program began giving the South Vietnamese government more responsibility for the conduct of the war. Vietnamization marked the beginning of a gradual drawdown in American strength.

A solid majority supported the war in 1965, but by 1968, the public's support for the war began to wane. The public's support fell to 35%.

The conflict was taking its toll on the political architects of the war. In 1968, President Johnson decided not to seek, nor to accept, his party's nomination for another term in office. North Vietnam's[3] leader, Ho Chi Minh, died of a heart attack the following year.

Armed Forces Radio Saigon began broadcasting soon after America's early involvement in the conflict. As additional stations in other cities throughout South Vietnam began broadcasting, the name was changed to American Forces Vietnam Network (AFVN). Early AFVN programming was unimaginative, dull, and seemed designed more as a sleep aid than a morale booster. In 1965, a young Air Force disk jockey changed everything.

"Gooood Morning, Vietnam" greeted listeners of AFVN's *Dawn Busters* program, and Sergeant Adrian Cronauer became an instant celebrity. Cronauer's tour in Vietnam was short, ending in 1966. His trademark "Gooood Morning, Vietnam," however, lived on, repeated by the troops long after the popular DJ's departure.

After reporting for duty to the commanding officer (CO) of Charlie Company, Bob Bauer, Mark Holtom, and Larry Wall settled into their quarters. During the

---

[3] The country commonly known as North Vietnam was formed as the Democratic Republic of Vietnam in 1945. After reunification with the South, the name was changed to the Socialist Republic of Vietnam on 2 July 1976.

transition to their strange new reality, the guys were beginning to appreciate the seriousness of their situation. The talk around the company area was all about a rocket attack that had devastated the company and taken the lives of three of their own.

The morning of 3 April 1970 was another hot, dusty day as Charlie Company prepared to fly the day's missions. Enlisted men were going about their morning routines—some were walking to or from the latrine, others were walking to the mess hall for breakfast, others still were already chowing down on eggs, greasy bacon, or chipped beef on toast, commonly referred to as S.O.S.[4]

The phrase, "another day in paradise" was undoubtedly exchanged, albeit with a chuckle between buddies, when their "paradise" was transformed into pure hell. Enemy 122 mm rockets began peppering the enlisted area of Charlie Company's compound.

The first enemy rocket hit the enlisted men's latrine, killing Staff Sergeant James Lee and Specialist Fourth Class (SP4) Ronald Parsons. Lee was the senior non-commissioned officer (NCO) in charge of the Second Flight Platoon and Parsons was the company's armorer. Both died instantly.

Rocket shrapnel or other flying debris hit seventeen other soldiers around the enlisted area. Their wounds ranged from minor to life-threatening. SP6 Richard Heath, the company's maintenance technical inspector,

---

[4] Chipped beef on toast is ground beef in flour gravy generally served over toast. It was commonly referred to as "Shit On a Shingle," or S.O.S.

died thirteen days later at an in-country hospital. Six others were eventually medevac'd to U.S. hospitals.

Hearing of the rocket attack of just a few days before their arrival brought home to Bauer, Holtom, and Wall the danger they would face during their next year in Vietnam. As FNG pilots, they knew that they would also be facing grave danger in the skies.

The North Flag flyers the guys met during their first days at Tay Ninh opened up and told them of the death of Charlie Company's CO just the month before.

Charlie Company's current CO, Captain Roger C. Baker, had recently replaced Captain William Lorimer, who had been killed on 10 March. Baker was just twenty-six years old and a junior captain when fate propelled him into the commander's position. Commanding the two-hundred-man Charlie Company was a big challenge, and Baker felt the pressure. He missed the friendship and guidance of his mentor terribly.

Captain Lorimer was a very popular commander, and he and the circumstances of his death were still widely discussed around the company.

Left to Right: Captain Roger "RC" Baker (top), Captain Bill Lorimer (bottom),
WO1 Robert "Jake" Jacobs and First Lieutenant Don "Thumpy" Thompson
Tay Ninh, circa January 1970
Lorimer was CO and Baker was XO of Charlie Company
Photo Courtesy of Roger Baker

www.roy-mark.com/Pics_Fixin/Lorimer2.jpg

The guys were told about the ill-fated mission that began routinely on the morning of 10 March 1970. An Army of the Republic of Vietnam (ARVN) battalion was in pursuit of the enemy. Charlie Company was called upon to extract the ARVNs from their current position and to transport them for insertion into a more favorable location. The ARVN commander had reported that the landing zone (LZ) was secure. Because no enemy troops were thought to be in the area, it would be a "cold extraction." For cold extractions, Cobra gunships accompanied the Hueys but did not pre-sweep the surrounding area with suppressing fire as they did for "hot extractions."

The mission called for a flight of seven Hueys, with First Lieutenant Don Thompson as mission commander. If, for any reason, it became necessary to split into two missions, Thompson would continue as mission commander of the first four Hueys and Dick Dunn would command the last three ships. Dunn would be the aircraft commander (AC) of Huey 7-7-2, the fifth ship of the flight.

Don Thompson was a Southern boy from Arkadelphia, Arkansas. Located about fifty-five miles southwest of Little Rock, Arkadelphia is a sleepy little college town with a good portion of the population consisting of students from the town's two universities. Henderson State University and Ouachita Baptist University also supply many of Arkadelphia's jobs.

When Thompson first arrived in Charlie Company in April of 1969, he immediately stood out from the crowd. Five foot six, with a gymnast's build, Thompson was the last person Hollywood would have cast as an Army pilot. Thompson was a little on the hyper side, and when he spoke, his Southern accent and hillbilly dialect immediately caught the attention of Charlie Company pilots. Thompson's flight leader took note of the hyper little FNG, who reminded him of the Disney cartoon character Thumper. Thumper was the rabbit that appeared in the film *Bambi* and was named for the way he thumped his hind paw. From this observation, Don was tagged with the nickname "Thumper." After a few days, "Thumper" had morphed into "Thumpy." Thompson quickly shook the FNG tag, but he remained Thumpy Thompson throughout his time in Vietnam.

On the mission to extract the ARVN troops, Thumpy would be flying a UH-1H with the tail number 68-16123. By then a flight leader himself, Thumpy had a designated ship assigned to him. He took possession of 1-2-3 in June 1969, soon after it arrived in-country. He flew 1-2-3 on a few missions before it, too, was also tagged with a nickname. Painted across the nose in white letters was *Thumpy 1*, the number 1 signifying Thumpy's status as flight leader.

UH-1H 68-16123 "Thumpy 1"
Photo Courtesy of Jack McCormick

www.roy-mark.com/Pics_Fixin/Thumpy_1.jpg

Dunn's co-pilot on the extraction mission would be Captain William Lorimer. Bill Lorimer was an excellent pilot, but flying was no longer his primary job. Captain Lorimer had been Charlie Company's executive officer (XO) until 15 February when he took over as CO. The men of Charlie Company liked and respected Captain Lorimer as their XO, and their respect for him increased during the weeks since he had assumed command. In his twenty-three days as CO, the responsibility of command kept him grounded much of the time, but he took every opportunity to join his men in the sky. Captain Lorimer's frequent forays into the skies with his men were just one of the reasons he was so well respected.

Bill Lorimer was actually William Lorimer IV. The first William Lorimer was Captain Lorimer's great-grandfather. William Lorimer[5] was a politician in Chicago in the late nineteenth and early twentieth centuries. He was elected to two nonconsecutive terms in the U.S. Congress and then was elected and served ten years as a U.S. senator from Illinois.

Captain Lorimer came from an Army family; his father retired as a full-bird colonel[6] and was living in Indiana. Being an Army brat[7], he and his two brothers and one sister grew up in many cities around the country. Bill Lorimer attended Saint John's Preparatory School in Collegeville, Minnesota, graduating in 1960. When he entered Saint John's University nearby, the name Bill Lorimer was already familiar to many of the freshman's professors; Bill's father, William Lorimer III, had been a professor of military science at Saint John's in the mid- to late 1950s. The younger Bill Lorimer earned a

---

[5] William Lorimer (27 April 1861 – 13 September 1934) was born in Manchester, England and immigrated with his family to the U.S. in 1866. The Lorimer family first settled in Michigan, but moved to Chicago in 1870.

[6] In the U.S. military, a colonel (O-6) is a field grade officer ranking just above lieutenant colonel (O-5). The colonel insignia is a silver eagle whereas the lieutenant colonel insignia is a silver oak leaf. Colonels are sometimes referred to (but not addressed) as "full-bird" colonels and lieutenant colonels as "light" colonels.

[7] The term Army brat describes a child of a parent serving in the Army; it refers to both current and former children of such families. It indicates moving to new states or countries many times while growing up as the family is customarily transferred to new assignments.

bachelor of science degree in social science in 1964. Lorimer was married during his senior year at Saint John's. He entered the Army shortly after graduation, and by 1970, when he became the commanding officer of Charlie Company, he and his wife had three young children. His wife and children were staying with his in-laws in Wheaton, Minnesota, while he was in Vietnam.

William Lorimer IV
Commanding Officer of Charlie Company, 229th Assault Helicopter Battalion
Captain Lorimer became CO in February 1970
Photo Compliments of Roger Baker
Captain Baker replaced Captain Lorimer as CO

www.roy-mark.com/Pics_Fixin/Lorimer1.jpg

The day began early for Thumpy Thompson and the men manning the seven Hueys of his flight. The mission sheet called for them to fly seven missions and seventy-three sorties to extract ARVN troops from their various positions and to insert them into new ones. Thumpy broke ground at 07:30 on that 10th day of March. By midday, they had flown two missions and fourteen sorties before shutting down for a quick lunch at Charlie Company's mess hall.

The third mission of the day began after lunch; Thumpy Thompson manned Huey 1-2-3, a.k.a. *Thumpy 1*, on the flight line at Tay Ninh and led the flight of seven Hueys into the Vietnamese skies. The short flight to the LZ would take about half an hour. They were escorted by two Cobra gunships from Delta Company. Known as "Smiling Tigers," Delta Company Cobras were a "don't leave home without" accessory for the lightly armed Hueys. Manning one of the Cobra escorts was Aircraft Commander (AC) WO1 Rod Barber and Peter-Pilot WO1 Lach Brown. As the flight approached the LZ, the seven Hueys began their descent, and the two Cobras began circling at eight-hundred feet to supply cover for the vulnerable Hueys. Captain Lorimer was at the controls of 7-7-2 as he and Dunn followed the first four Hueys into the LZ.

On the ground, with engines whining and dust flying, the ARVN troops were "elbows and assholes" as they climbed on board the seven Hueys. Crew chiefs and door-gunners supervised and assisted the ARVN grunts[8] as they threw their gear and themselves on board. By the time his crew chief gave the word that they were fully loaded, Dunn had lost track of how many ARVNs had boarded his ship, but he figured it was probably about eleven. He would normally carry only six or seven American grunts and their gear, but with ARVN soldiers being much smaller and carrying less gear than their

[8] Army slang for infantryman

American counterparts, a few extras could always be packed in. Everyone was anxious and ready to leave.

Pilots knew that they were very vulnerable on the ground, so it was always a relief to be leaving an LZ. They knew, too, that they were also quite vulnerable during approaches and departures from an LZ. The slow speed and low altitude during approaches and departures were a killer, literally a killer. They wouldn't rest easy until they were at altitude and out of range of small arms ground fire.

With the seven Hueys loaded, Thumpy led the exodus from the LZ. As *Thumpy 1* gained a little speed and altitude, Thompson began a turn to the left. The six other Hueys began following in succession.

The pilots of Army Hueys were protected by boron-carbon ceramic armor plates across their seatbacks and below their seats. Similar armor plating protected the right and left sides of the cockpit. The side armor was fitted on rails, allowing the heavy armor to slide forward and back for ease of entrance and exit. The armor plating around the cockpit gave pilots some protection on their sides, rear, and bottom, but the protection was far from complete. The Army provided additional protection for pilots and crew in the form of protective body armor. The body armor was made of boron carbide, silicon carbide, or aluminum oxide and was effective against small arms fire. Unlike the cockpit, the crew cabin had no armor plating. Crew members in the back had only their body armor—"chicken plates" as they were called—for protection. Chicken plates across their chest were effective against small arms fire coming at them horizontally, but not when fired from below.

For added protection, crews were issued thick ceramic plates to sit on. The plates were about one and a half inches thick and about fifteen inches square and encased in thick fabric with a strap for ease of handling. The plates undoubtedly were assigned a nomenclature by the Army, but the crews simply called them "butt plates." Butt plates were effective against small arms fire and could even stop a .51-caliber bullet. By whatever name, butt plates were known to have saved a crewmember's butt on occasion.

One of Charlie Company's crew chiefs, while flying at three-thousand feet, was unlucky enough to receive a .51-caliber round from below, but lucky enough to be sitting on his butt plate. The anti-aircraft round penetrated the bottom of his Huey and impacted his butt plate, launching him and his butt plate to a second impact with his Huey's ceiling. He survived the ordeal with a sore head, a sore neck, a sore ass, and great respect for his butt plate.

With the cabin's sliding doors still open and ARVN troops crammed into the back, Captain Lorimer lifted off, and Huey 7-7-2 began following the procession in a straight-out departure. It had been a routine extraction, as routine as any operation in a combat zone could possibly be; at five-hundred feet, that all changed.

Thumpy initiated his left turn at five-hundred feet, and the flight of Hueys began following in succession. When Lorimer's altimeter indicated five-hundred feet and with the first four Hueys at his nine o'clock position, he moved the cyclic stick to his left to initiate his left turn. Just then, several AK-47s began spraying the departing flight. With 7-7-2 banking in its left turn, Lorimer slumped and jerked the cyclic hard left. Panic gripped everyone on board as the Huey turned on its side. In the back, terror-stricken eyes looked through the open left door and saw solid ground where blue sky should be. With the floor of their Huey now vertical to the ground, the ARVN soldiers grabbed for anything they could to anchor themselves to the floundering Huey. One ARVN soldier reached out but grabbed only air. As he fell, his death wail was muted by the noise of the stricken Huey and the screams of his more fortunate comrades.

Huey 7-7-2 had rotated violently into an untenable position; by all rights, it should fall out of the sky. Dunn instinctively grabbed the stick even before his mind could assess the situation, and a precarious situation it was. With skill, luck, divine intervention, or copious portions of each, Dunn fought 7-7-2 back upright.

Rod Barber and Lach Brown were watching the entire flight from their Cobra gunship when they saw what they thought was one of the Hueys destined to crash. Barber immediately made a balls-on decision and descended to provide covering fire should there be any survivors of the crash. To their astonishment, the inevitable crash was averted. They marveled at the skill of the Huey pilot and vowed to stick with him to the end; if the Huey did eventually go down, they would need the protective firepower of a friendly Cobra.

Dunn's first priority was to save his ship. As he continued to fight the controls to keep 7-7-2 upright, a severe vibration began rattling everything, including all souls on board. He would learn later that the mast anchoring the main rotor was knocked out of kilter when the ship jerked violently on its side. The vibration was severe, and the situation bleak; keeping 7-7-2 in the air was dicey.

With Vietnam's horizon now horizontal instead of vertical across the windshield, Dunn began to gauge the situation. His pilot had been shot and was unconscious and slumped in his seat. His door-gunner, in his position near Lorimer, was on the intercom asking what he should do to help the CO. His Huey was still vibrating violently, he had lost control of his tail rotor, and now hydraulic pressure was beginning to fall. Hydraulic fluid was the lifeblood of the Huey; without it, controlling 7-7-2 would be next to impossible.

Dunn feared that Lorimer was losing his lifeblood too, so he directed his crew chief to stop the bleeding any way he could; stick his finger in the bullet hole if he had to, but stop the bleeding. Lorimer's wound was obviously very serious, but there wasn't much they could do now except to keep 7-7-2 in the air. Captain Lorimer needed immediate medical care, so Dunn pointed 7-7-2 in the direction of Tay Ninh and the base hospital.

Flight leader Thumpy Thompson notified Tactical Operations Center (TOC) of the situation, and TOC, in turn, notified the battalion's flight surgeon, Captain Craig Thomas. Doctor Thomas immediately headed for the 45th Surgical Hospital near the Tay Ninh runway; he would stand by for Lorimer's arrival.

It would take about thirty minutes to reach Tay Ninh if Dunn could keep 7-7-2 in one piece and in the air that long. He cut the flying time to Tay Ninh by coaxing every last knot[9] of forward airspeed out of the crippled bird. The velocity that should never be exceeded (VNE) on his UH-1H was 120 knots[10], and Dunn got every bit of that and maybe a little more out of 7-7-2 as they raced to Tay Ninh.

With a casualty on board a healthy bird, she could be landed on the helicopter pad next to the hospital, but 7-7-2 was far from healthy. In fact, without tail rotor control, landing on the helipad was completely out of the question; the only possibility of landing at all would be to initiate a gradual descent to the main runway. Dunn's approach would be more like a fixed-wing aircraft's.

Dunn was very familiar with the airport at Tay Ninh; it was, after all, his home base. He flew from Tay Ninh every day, and his hooch was near the runway, so he knew it was a huge sucker, about five-thousand feet long and very wide. The surface was covered with perforated steel planking (PSP). Runways could be built quickly and easily with PSP to make an acceptable landing strip for fixed-wing aircraft. Ironically, helicopter pilots never actually used the Tay Ninh runway; they landed on and departed from helicopter pads along its side. Dunn had passed over the runway thousands of

---

[9] A knot is a unit of speed equal to one nautical mile per hour or 1.151 miles per hour (1.852 kilometers per hour).
[10] 120 knots/hour is equivalent to about 138 miles per hour or 222 kilometers per hour.

times as he took off and landed. Now he was about to actually use it, albeit in an unconventional manner.

Huey 7-7-2 was approaching Tay Ninh from the north, and, knowing that the runway ran north and south, Dunn radioed the tower that he would be landing from the north. The tower advised him that the wind was from the north and that all traffic was landing from the south, into the wind. The tower then told him, with perhaps a hint of irritation, that a flight of C-130 cargo planes was on final from the south and that he would have to go around. With his hydraulics shot and no tail rotor control, going around for a south-to-north landing was not an option. He didn't have enough control of 7-7-2 to take her on a 180-degree tour of the countryside. Besides, he had to get his CO to the hospital and his bird on the ground before it vibrated itself out of the sky. Dunn didn't have the time or option to negotiate; he simply advised the tower, with a tone of authority in his voice, that he would be landing north to south. The tower, in the final analysis subservient to the pilot, diverted the C-130s and cleared 7-7-2 to land.

With minimal flight controls, slowing 7-7-2 down for a normal helicopter landing was completely out of the question. With skill, he managed to slow the crippled bird to about 126 miles per hour, but even so—in pilot jargon—he would be coming in "hot," very hot! To make matters worse, because Army Hueys were not fitted with wheels, 7-7-2 would land on its skids—no wheels, no brakes, and no directional control.

On the ground, soldiers in Tay Ninh's tower watched with apprehension as 7-7-2 approached the runway.

Barber and Brown had stuck close to 7-7-2, their Cobra's firepower ready to neutralize any threat. Now inside the base perimeter, their mission was completed. They could have flown their Cobra back to base, but they chose instead to shadow 7-7-2 all the way to touchdown.

Dunn touched down at the far northern end of the runway at about 126 miles per hour, and 7-7-2 began sliding on the PSP. He immediately shut down his engine and electrical systems; all on board were now just along for the ride. Pilot, crew, and passengers would end their harrowing journey at the mercy of 7-7-2. The metal skids screeched but offered little resistance against the steel PSP; it was like sliding on Teflon®[11].

Huey 7-7-2 was an injured bird, but a good bird. It was as if she put herself on autopilot and guided herself straight down the runway, but without brakes, she couldn't slow herself down. With little resistance, 7-7-2 and her passengers skidded down the runway like a puck on an air hockey table. Soldiers on the ground, unaware of the situation, were flabbergasted to see a Huey sliding down the runway. In the tower, everyone held their breath. By midfield, it was still balls-to-the-wall. About a quarter of the way from the end of the runway, Dunn began to sense a reduction in forward speed; 7-7-2 continued to skid and finally came to a labored halt. With no power and no control, 7-7-2 had skidded straight down four-fifths of the five-thousand-foot runway.

---

[11] Teflon® is a registered trademark of E.I. du Pont de Nemours and Company.

Looking down from their Cobra, Barber and Brown were awestruck; they not only watched a Huey pilot land a helicopter with no wheels, like a fixed-wing airplane, but they also saw 7-7-2 skid straight down the runway and end up as close to the hospital as possible. Non-pilots on the ground may not have been impressed, but the two highly skilled Cobra pilots watching from above knew they had just witnessed something remarkable. They landed their Cobra next to 7-7-2 to lend a hand.

When 7-7-2 finally came to a halt, the ambulance driver rushed to the stricken Huey, and Army medics removed Captain Lorimer from the right seat. Dunn jumped into the ambulance for the high-speed trip to the 45th Surgical Hospital a short distance away. The battalion's flight surgeon, Doctor Thomas, was standing by when the ambulance arrived at the emergency entrance.

The 45th Surgical Hospital was always a busy place; causalities came in every day. On this day, the hospital was especially busy. When Captain Lorimer was wheeled into the emergency room, all of the doctors were busy in operating rooms or looking after other critical patients. Doctor Thomas would have no support attending to his patient; nevertheless, he began his examination. He determined that, although unconscious, Lorimer's pupils were still pinpoint, which meant that there was still some blood circulating to the brain. There was a severe shortage of equipment at the time, so Doctor Thomas was unable to intubate his patient. He did manage to insert an IV to start fluids, but only by cutting down on

Lorimer's forearm to find a vein. Lorimer's veins were quite empty, indicating to the doctor that Lorimer had lost a massive amount of blood. Shortly thereafter, Captain William Lorimer IV succumbed to his wound and died.

Doctor Thomas had done all he could. Under ideal conditions, he might have been able to save the life of the man he considered his friend. Unfortunately, on that particular day, the conditions at 45th Surgical Hospital were far from ideal.

Back at 7-7-2, the crew was amazed at what they saw. The skids were burned away to practically nothing. As they examined the Huey for damage, they could see that the mast to the main rotor was clearly out of center. Search as they may, though, they could find not a single bullet hole anywhere on 7-7-2.

The bullet that killed their commanding officer was fired from the right rear as they were departing the LZ. It entered through the open sliding door behind Lorimer and passed by the door-gunner and ARVN troops, through the narrow gap between the armor plate behind his seat and the sliding armor panel protecting his right side. One inch to the right or left, and Lorimer would not have been scratched. The chance of a bullet following such a path was incalculable, a one-in-a-trillion tragedy.

Two days later, a memorial service was held for Captain Lorimer in Charlie Company's mess hall. The tables were removed, and extra chairs were brought in to accommodate everyone wanting to pay respects to their friend and commanding officer. Captain Lorimer's boots and helmet sat on a small table at the front of the makeshift chapel. At the end of the service, a seven-man firing squad fired a twenty-one-gun salute. Taps was then played for Captain William Lorimer IV, the 49,016th American to die in the Vietnam War.

Somewhere—probably mid-Pacific—Captain Lorimer's last letter to his wife, dated 9 March 1970, was making its way to Wheaton, Minnesota. The day before his death, Bill Lorimer wrote, "Hope things stay quiet today, they sure were hectic yesterday. Give my love to everyone."

The aviation skills of Dunn on that 10th day of March in 1970, were marveled at. Indeed, the actions of the entire crew of 7-7-2 were credited with saving the lives of many ARVN troops. In appreciation, the Army of the Republic of Vietnam awarded Dunn and the entire crew the Vietnamese Cross of Gallantry Medal with Gold Star.

One month later when Warrant Officers Bob Bauer, Mark Holtom, and Larry Wall arrived in Charlie Company, Captain Lorimer's death was still frequently discussed. There were slight variations with each telling, but the one constant was the use of the word "fluke." It just seemed so implausible that a single bullet could cause such a tragedy by finding that one-inch gap.

Soon after their arrival, Wall, Holtom, and Bauer completed check rides with Charlie Company's instructor pilot. The routine check rides behind them, the three immediately began flying their first true combat missions as Charlie Company peter-pilots.

Amidst the seriousness of war, the three new guys were soon introduced to the lighter side. The strict radio protocol they learned in flight school was not always followed to a tee. They soon heard other pilots key their radios and sing out, "Gooood Morning, Vietnam." Short-timers particularly reveled in announcing for all to hear, the number of days they had left in-country. "Gooood Morning, Vietnam" would crackle over the radio, followed by, "I'm short... ten days and a wake-up." If the short-timer was really short—less than ten days— he might announce that he was a "single-digit midget." Such rogue broadcasts were strictly unauthorized, but the jokester never used his call-sign, and it was, after all, a war-zone.

Bob Bauer and Mark Holtom's first flights were similar, but the outcomes, not so much. Bauer's first flights into combat seemed charmed. The bullets flew his way and there were close calls, but none seemed capable of finding their mark. Regardless of the aircraft commander he flew with, not a single bullet hole could be found in his Huey. In Army vernacular, Bauer didn't lose his cherry.

Holtom's first combat missions resulted in different outcomes. With Mark, finding bullet holes in his Huey after a mission became commonplace and testament to Holtom's loss of cherry. In fact, on 25 April, just a few days after he began flying for Charlie Company, Mark was wounded in action. He was peter-pilot on Huey 68-15240 at the time. Coincidentally, painted on the nose of 2-4-0 was a coiled snake and the name

"Snake Bit." Holtom's injuries weren't too serious, and he went flying the very next day.

The three FNGs' initiation into combat was truly jeopardous and at times downright frightening; that would not change. The pace of the action, however, did change with the coming of the Cambodian Incursion just days after their arrival in Charlie Company.

If Charlie Company's new pilots were anxious for action, they couldn't have arrived at a more opportune time. The Cambodian Incursion began just weeks after their arrival at Tay Ninh.

On 1 May, U.S. and South Vietnamese units entered Eastern Cambodia to attack the previously off-limits North Vietnamese and Viet Cong sanctuaries.

Intelligence estimated that approximately forty-thousand enemy troops had massed in the eastern border regions of Cambodia. During the operation, U.S. and ARVN forces overran the enemy and captured their supplies and arms. Thousands of enemy soldiers were killed, but U.S. forces suffered causalities as well.

When Bauer, Holtom, and Wall arrived in Charlie Company, they heard a lot of talk around the base about a pilot referred to as "The Ogre," or simply "Ogre." The Ogre was somewhat of a legend within Charlie Company, and the guys soon learned that the source of the legend was Chief Warrant Officer (CW2) Tom Agnew[12].

The nickname "Ogre" came from the mythical creatures of folklore and fiction, usually depicted as huge, hairy, humanoid beings with large heads, ample

---

[12] CW2 Thomas C. Agnew, 8 June 1946 – 11 November 1999

body hair, and voracious appetites. Captain Roger Baker, who was Charlie Company's XO at the time, said that Ogre was "a bit on the rotund side, had a big handlebar, and always had a shit-eating grin on his face and could put the fear of God in any FNG that dared enter the cockpit with him." The Ogres of folklore were often known to eat babies. The Ogre of Charlie Company didn't eat babies, but when one of The Ogre's FNG peter-pilots made a mistake, they may have been forgiven for believing the myth.

Tom "The Ogre" Agnew
Tay Ninh, January 1970
Photo Courtesy of CW2 Reg Baldwin

www.roy-mark.com/Pics_Fixin/Agnew_Tom.jpg

The Ogre's reputation was that of a fearless warrior. His reputation grew to legendary proportions one day in 1969. During an officers' meeting at Tay Ninh, the V.C.[13] began lobbing mortars into the base. Everyone dove for cover except Tom Agnew. The Ogre remained calmly in

---

[13] The North Vietnam sponsored National Liberation Front for South Vietnam was known in the South as "Viet Cong" or simply V.C. Using the military's phonetic alphabet, V.C. became "Victor Charlie" and its members became known as "Charlie."

his chair, nonchalantly sipping his beer. Carlton McKoy, a pilot present during that incredible event would later say of The Ogre, "He looked around at the other officers like we were all pussies." No one could help but respect The Ogre of Charlie Company. Tom Agnew commanded respected but was also very well liked around the Company.

In Vietnam, soldiers were billeted in quarters the troops referred to as a "hooch," and as a testament to The Ogre's popularity, the hooch he lived in was named "The Ogre's House."

Sign inside Tom "The Ogre" Agnew's hooch
229th Assault Helicopter Battalion Base at Tay Ninh
Photo Courtesy of CWO2 Calton McKoy

www.roy-mark.com/Pics_Fixin/Ogre-Plaque.jpg

Soon after Bob Bauer's arrival, the pilots that remembered The Ogre began to notice similarities between Bauer and The Ogre. Bauer's stature and appearance were not similar to Agnew's, but the similarity of his mannerisms cinched it; Bob Bauer became "Little Ogre."

Bob Bauer, at 23, was the oldest of the three and called Pearl River, New York, home. Mark Holtom was the product of both California and Kansas. Born in Hays, Kansas, Holtom spent his early years in Southern California in and around Long Beach before returning to Kansas as a teen. In Ellinwood, Kansas, Holtom lived with an aunt and uncle and attended Ellinwood High School. Mark played football, ran track, was active in the school's Latin Club, and was an honor student. After graduation, Mark attended the University of Kansas for a year before joining the Army to fly helicopters. He arrived in South Vietnam ready to fly helicopters just four days after his twenty-first birthday.

3 GOING UP THE COUNTRY

Two weeks into the Cambodian Incursion and things were going well for Charlie Company. Everyone was putting in long hours. Days began early and ended late; it was sometimes after dark when the last Huey returned to base.

Twenty-two-year-old Chief Warrant Officer (CW2) Neil Blume started his day early on Friday, 15 May 1970. The day began hot, and as with most days in Vietnam during the month of May, the early-morning heat was a harbinger of scorching temperatures to come. On his way to breakfast, Blume stopped by the TOC and learned he had been assigned a Command and Control[14] (C&C) mission into Cambodia. On a C&C mission, Blume knew that he would be flying the commanding officer of one of the field units.

Blume's personal call sign was "Beeper"; he was known as Beeper not only in the air, but around the base

---

[14] Command and Control is the exercise of authority and direction by a commanding officer over his forces in the accomplishment of the mission.

as well. Neil Blume grew up just outside the small Minnesota farming community of Herman[15]. The entire area of Herman is hardly one square mile with a population of less than five-hundred folks. Herman is so small, it doesn't even have the typical small town amber caution light to slow the occasional car or truck passing through town. The small community in the western portion of the state known as Vikingland sits about 167 miles northwest of Minneapolis and 85 miles southeast of Fargo, North Dakota.

Neil attended Herman Community School for twelve years and graduated with forty-one other seniors. In high school, he was on his school's wrestling team, and he continued that pursuit when he went off to college at the University of Minnesota Technical College at Crookston[16]. In Crookston, Neil took time from his studies and athletics to pursue a dream: he learned to fly and got his single-engine fixed-wing private pilot's license.

After earning an associate's degree in agriculture engineering, Neil's interest in aviation led him to the Army, where he hoped to go to flight school. When Neil enlisted in 1968, his Army recruiter had offered no guarantees, so he was pleased when he learned he had been assigned to flight training at the Army's Primary

---

[15] Herman, MN, was the subject of the 2001 film, *Herman U.S.A.* Inspired by a true story, *Herman U.S.A.* is a comedy starring Kevin Chamberlin, Michael O'Keefe, and Enid Graham.

[16] The University of Minnesota Technical Institute became the University of Minnesota, Crookston in 1988.

Helicopter Training Center at Fort Wolters, Texas. Neil would become a helicopter pilot.

Neil "Beeper" Blume
Vietnam, 1970
Photo Compliments of Roger "RC" Baker

www.roy-mark.com/Pics_Fixin/Blume_Neil.jpg

At Tay Ninh, "Beeper" Blume made his way to the flight line and again scanned his mission sheet. He saw that he would be flying Huey 68-15728, and that his peter-pilot would be WO1 William Grant. Their door-gunner on 7-2-8 would be SP4 John Stinn. Stinn was actually a last minute change to the mission sheet. SP5 John "PJ" Pecha was originally scheduled as 7-2-8's door-gunner.

Pecha's friends had tagged him with "PJ" because it was easier on the tongue than Pecha. PJ was not a regular door-gunner; his regular job as aircraft electrician and instrument repairman kept him busy keeping the Hueys' electronics and special equipment in proper working order. Months before, when Charlie Company found itself critically short of personnel in the flight platoons, PJ answered an urgent call for volunteers. He continued with his regular job, but was called upon occasionally to fly as door-gunner, usually on C&C missions. C&C missions were generally considered less dangerous than were combat assault missions. Since Blume's mission for 15 May was a C&C, the Flight Platoon Sergeant requested SP5 Pecha to fill the door-gunner assignment; PJ readily agreed.

SP4 John Stinn had returned to Tay Ninh just days before from a temporary assignment. He had been working at a remote firebase loading rockets onto Cobra helicopters. Upon his return, he requested a transfer to a flight platoon as door-gunner. It took a few days for his request to be processed, but by the morning of 15 May, Stinn was officially listed as a door-gunner.

As "PJ" Pecha was preparing for the mission, he was told he wouldn't be needed; Stinn was back and would fly the mission.

Twenty-year-old John Stinn was from Panama, a small town in Southwest Iowa with a population of just 221 souls. Panama was one of many small towns in the rural county of Shelby. The entire population of Shelby County was no more than most small towns in America, just 15,528 when the census was taken earlier in 1970. The nearest large cities are Omaha, Nebraska to the southwest, and Des Moines to the east. Many of John's neighbors back in Shelby County were, like himself, Roman Catholic of Germanic descent. John had two brothers and two sisters. Another sister had died of kidney disease when John was just five years old. If asked how many cousins he had, Stinn would have a hard time counting them all, but they totaled somewhere north of forty, just in Shelby County alone. It was a close-knit extended family with most of John's many aunts, uncles, and cousins living within twenty miles or so.

John Stinn attended college for a while, but when faced with the prospect of being drafted, decided to enlist instead; problem was, the Army's minimum enlistment was for three years, and John was anxious to get his military obligation behind him. The local Army recruiter offered a solution that John found acceptable; he would volunteer to be drafted, thereby reducing his obligation. He would be back in Shelby County with his family and steady girlfriend in just two years.

The first part of their mission that day—the easy part—required Blume and his crew to fly the approximate forty-seven miles to the 1st Cavalry's headquarters in Phuoc Vinh. There, they would pick up the commanding officer of the 8th Engineer Battalion.

As Beeper approached Huey 7-2-8, he was pleased to see that preparations for the mission were underway by his crew. Peter-Pilot Grant was finishing up with the radio checks and his crew chief and door-gunner had their M-60 machine guns mounted and prepped. The routine was familiar to everyone, except Door-Gunner Stinn.

John Stinn had been in-country eight months, so he was no new guy. Nevertheless, as the engine of Huey 68-15728 began to whine on the tarmac at Tay Ninh, Stinn was undoubtedly anxious, excited, and perhaps a little nervous; he was flying his first combat mission.

SP4 Stinn had been working those eight months in an administrative position. Among his other duties, Stinn often delivered the company mail. John particularly enjoyed taking mail to the guys in the flight platoons. Not only did it give him the opportunity to get out of the orderly room for a while, he enjoyed the interaction with all the guys of Charlie Company.

Perhaps it was the stories told by the door-gunners and crew chiefs and their friendly ribbing, or perhaps it was a yearning deep within, but John Stinn wanted to fly. His request for transfer to a flight platoon was granted and now Door-Gunner John Stinn was primed and pumped to begin his first mission.

Peter-Pilot Grant was in his seat on the right side of the Huey when Beeper entered through the left door. He adjusted his seat and then slid the armor plating forward on his left side. The armor plating served a vital purpose, but limited access to the cockpit.

As the Huey climbed to altitude, the crew began feeling the cooler air circulating through the cabin. Grant tuned one of the AM radios to AFVN; a little Rock-n'-Roll seemed in order for the half-hour flight.

At Phuoc Vinh, they picked up the commanding officer of the 8th Engineer Battalion, Lieutenant Colonel Scott Smith, and two of the battalion's recon sergeants. Smith was a career soldier, a "lifer" in the parlance of the flight crew that met him on the tarmac at Phuoc Vinh.

Lieutenant Colonel Scott Smith, 1970
Photo Courtesy of Major General Scott Smith

www.roy-mark.com/Pics_Fixin/Smith_Scott.jpg

Smith, now 35 years old, was considered an old man by the teenage and twenty-something soldiers he commanded. In fact, as with most commanding officers, he was often referred to as "The Old Man" by his men.

Born in Buffalo, New York, to Canadian parents, Scott Smith was raised in Connecticut, not far from the U.S. Military Academy (USMA) at West Point, New York. As a boy, Smith admired the Academy and the Cadets, so he was thrilled in 1952 to receive an appointment to the USMA. Upon graduation in 1956, Smith was commissioned a second lieutenant in the Corps of Engineers.

Smith, now a Lieutenant Colonel, was serving his third tour in Vietnam. One of Smith's fellow Class of 1956 graduates, Norman Schwarzkopf[17], Jr., was also serving in Vietnam. Schwarzkopf was Commanding Officer of the 1st Battalion, 6th Infantry, 198th Infantry Brigade at Chu Lai. Many years later, Schwarzkopf would command coalition forces in evicting Saddam Hussein's Army from neighboring Kuwait.

Colonel Smith, with the two recon sergeants, Staff Sergeant Arnold Robbins[18] and Sergeant Melvin Thomas, approached the waiting Huey with an air of authority. Robbins—from Bravo Company—took a seat at the starboard (right) door behind Peter-Pilot Grant and next to Door-Gunner Stinn. Thomas was from the battalions' Headquarters and Headquarters Company; he entered Huey 7-2-8 and took his seat at the center of the bench seat. Thomas carried a sawed-off 12 gauge and Robbins held his M-16 by his side. Smith, with his .38 caliber revolver strapped to his side, entered last and took his place just behind Aircraft Commander Beeper Blume. They felt sufficiently armed for the day's C&C mission.

Arnold Robbins entered the Army in 1952, in time to see action in the Korean War. Now, with eighteen years of service and two wars under his belt, he could look forward to his well-deserved retirement offered by the Army after twenty years of service. With less than a month to go before his tour in Vietnam was completed,

---

[17] H. Norman Schwarzkopf, 22 August 1934 – 27 December 2012
[18] Arnold Lee Robbins was posthumously promoted to Sergeant First Class.

Robbins was also looking forward to returning to his wife and son at their Salamanca, New York, home.

Twenty-year-old Melvin Thomas may have been considered young to be a Sergeant; his chevrons were the result of his proficiency and devotion to duty. In fact, he had just recently extended his tour in Vietnam, and now had over 14 months in-country. Thomas was from Ada, Michigan, a small town just east of Grand Rapids.

The Cambodian Incursion was into its third week and progress was good. With progress came the need to build firebases, and Smith's 8th Engineer Battalion was critical to the planning and later construction process. Smith's mission objective was to survey three potential firebase sites. He wanted to evaluate the size of each and to check for proximity to running water. The recon sergeants would determine the depth of the water table and other technical factors that were vital if a firebase were to be successful. Smith also wanted to visit four or five other locations where engineering help had been requested. Infantry and artillery units often needed help crossing obstacles and building protective berms. The 8th Engineer Battalion was even called upon at times to blow up captured North Vietnamese Army (NVA) rice stores. Later in the day, Smith hoped to visit a couple of his 8th Engineer units in the field. Beeper Blume and the flight crew knew they were in for a long hard day; they'd be lucky to see the inside of their hooches before dark.

After lifting off from Phuoc Vinh, they flew toward Cambodia, but before leaving Vietnam airspace, they made a refueling stop at the Army air base at Song Be.

The Song Be base was near the border and was their last chance for fuel before beginning the mission inside Cambodia. The 242 gallons of the Huey's five connected fuel cells would be necessary on this mission; aviation fuel was not readily available inside Cambodia.

It was still early, about 09:00, when Huey 7-2-8 approached the first site. Beeper keyed his intercom and directed Smith's attention to a clearing. Smith looked down and did a quick visual of a rectangular-shaped field about a hundred meters long.

Needing a closer inspection, Smith directed Beeper to land. Blume circled the clearing and the crew scanned closely for any signs of enemy activity. They did see activity, but it was friendlies a couple of klicks[19] from the clearing.

On the ground, a rifle company of the 12th Cavalry looked up as the familiar "thump thump thump" announced the approach of a Huey. Eyeballs followed the Huey as it circled and then descended over the treetops. They knew the Huey was landing at the clearing near where they had camped the night before.

The Huey descended into the clearing and Beeper brought the Huey to a hover in preparation for landing. Off to the right, unseen by Beeper Blume or Peter-Pilot Grant, an NVA soldier raised his rocket-propelled grenade[20] (RPG[21]) and took aim at what he must have considered a tempting and irresistible target.

---

[19] In military slang, a "klick" is a kilometer or 1,000 meters. One kilometer equals .621371 miles.

[20] A shoulder-fired weapon system that fires rockets equipped with an explosive warhead.

Door-Gunner Stinn was first to see the threat; he simultaneously raised the alarm on the intercom and swung his M-60 toward the enemy. Stinn opened fire just as the RPG was launched. Others in the back of the Huey instinctively looked to Stinn as he began blazing away with his M-60. Events seemed to be unfolding in slow-motion. They watched in horror as the missile approached, growing larger and larger until it slammed into the fuel cell to Stinn's right. A terrific explosion rocked the Huey and a fireball erupted; 7-2-8 settled violently to the ground and was engulfed in flames.

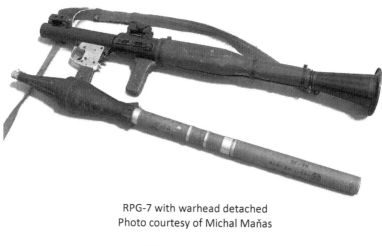

RPG-7 with warhead detached
Photo courtesy of Michal Maňas

www.roy-mark.com/Pics_Fixin/RPG-7.jpg

---

[21] RPG is an initialism from the Russian language which translates to "hand-held anti-tank grenade launcher." Thus, "rocket-propelled grenade" is an acronym.

When the RPG hit near Stinn, Colonel Smith and the crew chief were sitting on the opposite side of the Huey. Smith had his legs outside the cabin in preparation for landing; the concussion hurled him free of the fireball and slammed him violently to the ground. The crew chief managed to escape through the left side door.

Peter-Pilot Grant jumped out as Beeper Blume keyed his mike and broadcast, "Mayday" on the emergency frequency[22]. With fire raging around him, Beeper hastily gave his call sign and general location before trying to exit the inferno. Panic struck as he realized he couldn't get his armor plating to slide back; he was trapped in a burning Huey.

Fire engulfed 7-2-8; the heat was intense. Suddenly, 7.62-millimeter rounds from the two M-60 machine guns began cooking off on both sides of the Huey. Thomas' 12 gauge and Robbins' M-16, which were still inside the burning Huey, joined in the chaos; lead was flying in all directions. In the mayhem, Grant saw that Beeper was having problems getting out, so he came around to the pilot's side and physically pulled Beeper out by the collar of his flight suit.

Smith would later say, "With all the various rounds cooking off, I at first thought we were under attack by an enemy battalion." It took a moment to assess the situation. They were not under attack, but an attack might be eminent.

In the panic and confusion of the moment, they weren't sure how they got out of the burning wreck, but

---

[22] The emergency frequency of 121.5 MHz, referred to as "Guard" by the Army, was monitored by all aircraft.

there they were, some standing, some sitting and some prone on the ground.

Fearing an attack, the walking survivors surveyed their situation. SP4 Stinn was dead. Sergeants Robbins and Thomas were severely wounded and barely conscious. Beeper and Grant were burned on their necks, but thanks to their fire-resistant flight suits, were otherwise fine. Smith and the crew chief were shaken up and had minor injuries, but were fit to fight. Their problem was, they had very little to fight with.

Inside their Huey were the burned remnants of two M-60 machine guns, an M-16, and a sawed-off 12 gauge. The four walking survivors faced a feared enemy attack with just three .38 caliber revolvers; they were not reassured.

The RPG shooter was gone and the feared attack never came. They had no idea if anyone heard Beeper's Mayday call, or for that matter if the radio signal actually left the burning Huey. Not knowing if help was on the way, they figured their best bet was to hike down a trail toward the infantry company they had seen as they circled the clearing. They headed down the trail, cautious of mines as they walked. After about thirty minutes of walking, they were relieved to meet Americans soldiers coming in their direction.

The grunts on the ground had heard the explosion and seen a column of black smoke ascending. They knew the Huey they had seen circling had crashed in the clearing, so they headed in that direction to see if they could help. The rifle company of the 12th Cavalry and their firepower were a welcome sight to the survivors.

The 12th Cavalry soldiers escorted the crew and Smith back to the crash site and assisted in the medevac. At the aid station, Staff Sergeant Arnold Robbins was pronounced dead. Sergeant Melvin Thomas was treated, but his injuries were too severe; he died later that day.

A memorial service for SP4 John Richard Stinn was held in the company mess hall. Everyone in Charlie Company remembered John as their friendly, outgoing mail clerk. Now they sat in solemn respect at the memorial of Door-Gunner John Stinn. They listened to words about duty, sacrifice, and courage under fire. They had lost a comrade and a friend.

John Stinn
Photo Courtesy of John Stinn's Family

www.roy-mark.com/Pics_Fixin/Stinn-1.jpg

www.roy-mark.com/Pics_Fixin/Stinn-2.jpg

SP4 Stinn was Charlie Company's first loss during the Cambodian Incursion; as a bugler played taps, they dared to hope he would be the last.

At Phuoc Vinh, 8th Engineer Battalion's Headquarters and Headquarters Company held a memorial service for Staff Sergeant Arnold Lee Robbins. At Fire Support Base (FSB) Buttons, about thirty minutes flying time north of Phuoc Vinh, Bravo Company, 8th Engineer Battalion held a solemn service in memory of Sergeant Melvin Ray Thomas.

Taps sounded at FSB Buttons, at Phuoc Vinh, and at Tay Ninh that day. Around South Vietnam, other memorial services were held in chapels, mess halls, and open fields for the thirteen others—ten Soldiers, two Marines, and one Sailor—killed on Friday, 15 May 1970.

The following Sunday—half a world away—Iowa awoke to the usual sounds of church bells. Panama was a tight-knit religious community where everyone was on speaking terms with their parish priest. When the doorbell rang at Alfred and Catherine Stinn's residence, nothing seemed amiss. A visit by their parish priest was not at all unusual, but when the Stinns saw the crestfallen stranger in full Army uniform, words need not be spoken. John Stinn's mother collapsed into her priest's embrace with uncontrollable sobs.

After the loss of SP4 Stinn, Charlie Company grieved but continued the fight. Unlike the assessment of the news media back in the world, the guys actually doing the fighting knew they were kicking ass and taking names. The kicker, however, was about to become the kickee; another enemy was about to conduct a reality check.

4 FIRE AND RAIN

Twenty-seven days after the loss of John Stinn, the Cambodian Incursion, not to mention the men of Charlie Company, was still going balls to the wall. North Flag flyers were grinding out missions from zero dark thirty in the morning till well after dark. The daily routine became wake up, fly, get a few hours of fitful sleep, wake up, and fly again.

Although the daily grind became routine, no single mission could ever be considered routine; there was nothing routine about combat during the Cambodian Incursion. Bullets flying and men dying—both bad and good—could never be considered routine.

On 11 June 1970, WO1 James Bulloch was tasked with flying a mission into Cambodia in support of 8th Engineer Battalion, who were themselves supporting infantry and artillery elements of the 1st Cavalry Division inside Cambodia.

Bulloch would be flying Huey 66-16985 with SP4 Raymond Uhl as crew chief and SP4 Alonzo Taylor as his door-gunner. The only aspect slightly out of the ordinary as 9-8-5 lifted off from Tay Ninh that Thursday morning was that the battalion's safety officer—a lieutenant—would be flying with Bulloch as co-pilot.

Jim Bulloch was occasionally referred to as "Big Jim" by close friends, not because he was big in stature—he wasn't—it was just a tag that stuck somewhere along the way. Born in 1938 in Georgia, the now 32-year-old was one of the oldest pilots in Charlie Company. Big Jim also had more time in the Army than any of the other pilots. He enlisted soon after his eighteenth birthday, and by the time circumstances had brought him to Vietnam, he had served at bases around the United States and a three-year tour in Schweinfurt, Germany. Bulloch served as an enlisted man in the years leading up to the Vietnam War, earning a sleeve full of chevrons along the way. When the Army offered Jim the opportunity to train as a helicopter pilot, he jumped at the opportunity.

Bulloch was a short-timer; his arrival in-country almost eleven months earlier seemed like a lifetime ago. By now, Jim had earned the right to greet each morning, like this morning by announcing to his hooch mates, "twenty-seven days and a wake up!" Being the quiet type, Jim probably just smiled and uttered the traditional "good morning."

Bulloch now called Albuquerque home, and home was undoubtedly on his mind where his wife and two daughters were counting the days until his return.

Late in the afternoon of 11 June, after a very long day of flying missions inside Cambodia, Bulloch and his crew finally crossed back into Vietnam airspace. They were headed home but had to make a stop in Phuoc Vinh to drop off their 8th Engineer passengers. They landed at Phuoc Vhin with dusk falling rapidly; the sun had set about 6:15 that evening.

Once on the ground at Phuoc Vinh, Bulloch's co-pilot—slash battalion safety officer—said that he would stay at Phuoc Vinh overnight in order to attend a safety meeting there the next day. As aircraft commander, the ultimate authority to release his co-pilot lay squarely on Bulloch's shoulders. Doing so, however, was a tough call politically since the co-pilot was a lieutenant and outranked Warrant Officer Bulloch.

With the co-pilot seat now empty, Crew Chief SP4 Raymond Uhl jumped at the rare opportunity and requested permission to ride in the cockpit with his AC. Bulloch granted permission, and Uhl eagerly left the back of 9-8-5 in the capable hands of Door-Gunner SP4 Alonzo Taylor.

Twenty-one-year-old Uhl was from Denver, Colorado, and came from a very large family of nine brothers and sisters. Ray Uhl graduated from George Washington High School before entering Metropolitan State College in Denver. Before dropping out of college, he had taken a few flight lessons and attended ground school. After college, there was the ominous shadow of the draft.

For Raymond Uhl, enlisting was not an option; the three or four year commitment would keep him away from his steady girl too long. He considered it better to be drafted; two years was better than three or four.

After boot camp and completing the Army's helicopter maintenance course at Fort Rucker, Alabama, Uhl was sent to Vietnam. He had been in-country just twenty-one days and in Charlie Company barely a week. To the Army, Uhl was a fully qualified crew chief; to his peers, he was another new guy.

Bulloch would be carrying three passengers back to Tay Ninh. Door-Gunner Taylor, now the lone crewman in the back, assisted the passengers onboard.

Fellow North-Flagger Franklin Meyer was a familiar face to Taylor. Meyer was a helicopter mechanic for Charlie Company and flew occasionally; service calls were just part of the job. To say that Meyer was from a small town would be an understatement; the population of Smicksburg, Pennsylvania, could be counted on the fingers of five residents. Smicksburg is an Amish community[23] about seventy miles northeast of Pittsburg. Meyer was just eighteen and a half years old. After enlisting and completing boot camp, he trained as a helicopter mechanic before being sent to Vietnam. Meyer was still considered a new guy, having been in-country barely a month.

The other two passengers to Tay Ninh were SP4 John Dossett and SP4 Vernon Bergquist. Both were from Alpha Company and both were Mid-Westerners; Bergquist was from Spencer, Iowa, and Dossett was from Lamar, Missouri. Nineteen-year-old Dossett had graduated from Lamar High School in 1969 and, like Meyer, was a trained helicopter mechanic.

---

[23] Franklin Delano Meyer's religion was recorded by the Army as Methodist (also Evangelical Brethren).

Twenty-one-year-old Bergquist worked as an Alpha Company supply specialist.

SP4 Alanzo Taylor, who was now the de-facto crew chief, manned his M-60 machine gun and insured that all passengers were onboard. Twenty-one-year-old Taylor was from Pomona, near Los Angeles, California. He was a helicopter mechanic but had completed in-country training to become a door-gunner. He now was acting crew chief, a position he hoped, and expected to be, promoted to in the near future.

As helicopter repairmen, both Dossett and Taylor were called upon to fly occasionally; during the Cambodian Incursion, those occasions arose more frequently. As a supply specialist for Alpha Company, Bergquist didn't fly as often, but the situation now called for everyone to pitch in.

After refueling at Phuoc Vinh, Bulloch flew the short distance to Dau Tieng and joined two other Charlie Company Hueys and one Alpha Company Huey for the final leg of their journey home to Tay Ninh. The gaggle of four ships would be led by Flight Leader WO1 Steve Reed in Huey 7-4-5. While still on the ground, and from his position inside 7-4-5's cockpit, Reed surveyed the other three ships of his gaggle and made radio contact. All was well, and Reed observed nothing unusual. He expected the night flight to take about thirty minutes.

With the four ship gaggle formed and everyone anxious to get home to Tay Ninh, 9-8-5 lifted off about seven-thirty that evening into already dark skies.

In Tay Ninh, the weather was beginning to act up. The monsoon season had begun a few weeks earlier, and along with it came frequent and severe late-afternoon thunderstorms. The winds at Tay Ninh began picking up, and the already dark skies became black.

Concerned for his three ships that had not yet returned from their missions, Charlie Company CO Captain Roger Baker went to his TOC to check on their status. His operations officer, Captain Kirk Sharrock, reported that the three Charlie Company ships along with one Alpha ship were en route to Tay Ninh.

In the sky, the four-ship gaggle ran into bad weather that seemed to get worse by the minute; they were entering the same thunderstorm that hit Tay Ninh a few minutes before. At Tay Ninh, conditions could only be described as severe. The driving rain and gusting winds made for very hazardous flying conditions; in fact, no Huey should be flying in that weather.

Captain Sharrock radioed a weather warning to the gaggle with instructions to return to Phuoc Vinh if conditions were too severe. Flight Leader WO1 Steve Reed roger'ed that message. The operations center was tense; Captain Baker and his men waited as the storm showed no signs of moderating.

In the sky, the gaggle entered the worst of the storm, and the driving rain immediately reduced visibility to near nothing. Reed was more than a little worried; four ships flying in close formation with virtually zero visibility was a disaster in the making. In such conditions, a mid-air collision was a real possibility; just the mention of "mid-air" was enough to make any aviator's knees turn to jelly. Reed got on the radio and directed Bulloch in 9-8-5 and the Alpha ship (0-9-5) to divert to the right, south of the storm while he and Schaefer in 5-7-1 would divert to the left. Splitting the gaggle would at least reducing the risk of a mid-air.

Schaefer diverted to the north; visibility was zero and the wind threatened to abruptly end his flight with each gust. At times he had to apply full power, and even then the wind was forcing him down at fifteen-hundred feet per minute. Without visual references, his training kicked in and he began flying strictly by his instruments.

In the operations center, the minutes passed and the tension mounted. Suddenly, at about 8:15, a Huey came in at low level right over the company area. There was a brief moment of relief as they saw that it was WO1 Reed, the flight leader in 7-4-5. Nerves tensed again with the realization that 7-4-5 was alone; three Hueys were still out there fighting the storm. Abruptly, the radio crackled to life again with a panicked voice:

"Get off the controls, get off the controls!"

Was that 9-8-5? They weren't sure but thought so; It sounded like Bulloch's voice, but they weren't sure. Captain Sharrock began calling Bulloch's Huey, "9-8-5, North Flag Three[24], over… 9-8-5, North Flag Three, over…" Again and again they called; again and again the response was dead silence.

Finally a response! It was WO1 Joe Schaefer[25] in 5-7-1 reporting that he had diverted to the north—clear of the

---

[24] Charlie Company's radio call sign was "North Flag" and operations were designated, "G-3"; therefore, the operations officer's radio call sign was "North Flag Three."

storm—and would be landing shortly. He said that he, too, had heard the panicked radio call and that it must have been 9-8-5 . With the storm waning, Schaefer made it back to base safely a few minutes later.

In the TOC, Captain Baker notified battalion headquarters of the fluid situation. As he spoke, the third Huey, Alpha Company's 0-9-5 landed at the north end of the field near Alpha Company's area. With just one Huey unaccounted for, it had to be Bulloch in 9-8-5. Then battalion called with the devastating news that they had received a report of a crash to the southeast.

Captain Baker had alerted his Nighthawk crew, and they had the Nighthawk Huey standing by for a search and rescue mission. Nighthawk was a modified Huey with a large fifty-thousand watt search light and starlight scope—a night vision device—mounted on the left side, just forward of the crew chief; it would be ideal for a nighttime search and rescue mission.

Captain Baker and WO1 Mark Panageotes rushed to the flight line and manned the Nighthawk. As they lifted off toward the southeast, the rain continued to restrict visibility. Conditions were far from ideal for the search, but battalion soon called with a more accurate estimate of a possible crash site.

With the search area narrowed, they soon located the crash site. Hearts sank as they realized there would be no rescue; what appeared in the bright searchlight was the result of a violent crash into a rice paddy. Baker landed his Nighthawk and called for ground forces to

---

[25] Joseph E. Schaefer III, 14 January 1948 — 10 January 2005

come and secure the area. Waiting for the ground forces to arrive, they looked over the wreckage and saw that there had been a small explosion; small fires were still burning. They couldn't help but cringe at the total and utter devastation resulting from the high speed impact into the ground.

* * *

The next morning dawned as any other except that Charlie Company awoke to the realization that they had lost three of their own—lost to the nastiest thunderstorm most had yet seen in Vietnam. It was Monday, 12 June 1970 and the beginning of a new work-week back in the world. For the guys at Tay Ninh, Vietnam, one day was much like any other: missions were assigned and flown from early morning till after dark, and occasionally good men died.

For Warrant Officer Les Tatarski, 12 June was to be a special day; this was to be the beginning of his R&R[26]and a rendezvous with his wife in Hawaii. It was not to be. His wife called a few days before, told her husband that she was sick, and asked if they could delay their reunion in Hawaii until after she recovered. Tatarski went to his CO, Captain Roger Baker with a request to reschedule his R&R. Baker considered Tatarski to be a quiet, serious young man and a different cut from the average young

---

[26] R&R is military slang for rest and recuperation (alternately, rest and relaxation or rest and recreation). There were R&R destinations in Southeast Asia such as Bangkok, Manila, and Singapore among others. Other, more far-flung destinations included Tokyo, Sydney, and Hawaii.

warrant pilot; Tatarski's request was immediately approved. Tatarski was disappointed of course; he was looking forward to a visit with his wife and their new baby he had not yet seen. Just as well, though, their visit would be so much better after his wife's recovery.

Warrant Officer Les Tatarski was from Buffalo, New York, and had been in-country for over ten months. He had been an aircraft commander for much of those ten months and had flown some hairy missions; he was expecting today's missions into Cambodia to be more of the same.

Nicknames are common throughout the military, and for someone with a name like Tatarski, being called "Ski" was to be expected, but some of his close friends tagged Tatarski with a more imaginative nickname. His closest friend and hooch mate, Joe Schaefer, along with Dan Tyler and a few others began calling Tatarski "Tango." The Tango tag came from the military's phonetic alphabet; the letter "T" is pronounced "Tango," and Tango rolled off the tongue far easier than "Tatarski."

Instead of flying out of Vietnam on R&R as he had been expecting, WO1 Les "Tango" Tatarski would be flying another mission. Instead of meeting his wife in Hawaii, he would meet the enemy in the "Fishhook"[27] region of Cambodia.

Tango's mission was to re-supply paratroopers of 11 Company of the ARVN's 1st Airborne Battalion, Airborne Division. They were critically short of ammo

---

[27] The "Fishhook" was the name given to an area of Southeast Cambodia approximately 50 miles (80 kilometers) northwest of Saigon (present day Ho Chi Minh City).

and medical supplies for their large number of wounded, and—just as importantly—they were completely out of smoke grenades. Without smoke to mark their location, resupply missions—including this one—would be more difficult.

The ARVN unit was in desperate need of another critical item. The American advisor that had accompanied them into Cambodia had been killed; Tatarski's mission called for dropping off supplies and for inserting a replacement advisor as well. The new advisor—a U.S. Army lieutenant—would be accompanied by Major Robert Bailey. Bailey was the ARVN battalion's senior advisor. After inserting his lieutenant and evaluating the situation, Bailey would return to Vietnam with Les Tatarski.

Tango scanned his mission sheet and saw that he would be flying Huey 68-15240. The nose art on 2-4-0 announced its arrival to its adversaries with a painting of a coiled black snake above the words "Snake Bit." Snake Bit had another, albeit unofficial nickname. Snake Bit's enlisted crew took to calling her "The Magnet" because of her history of attracting ground fire.

Tango was pleased to see that his peter-pilot would be WO1 Larry Wall, one of the most experienced and competent pilots in Charlie Company. Wall was fulfilling a boyhood desire to fly helicopters. As a boy growing up in Southern California, young Larry Wall lived near the Marine Corps Air Station at El Toro. His house was near the flight path of the departing and landing Marine helicopters. Watching those helicopters must have sparked the urge, or ignited an innate desire in the boy to one day become a helicopter pilot himself. That desire simmered throughout his high school years at La Quinta High School in Westminster where he played football and was a shot putter on the track and field team. Wall attended Orange Coast Community College in Costa Mesa for one semester. When the Army promised him helicopter flight school, Wall jumped at the opportunity.

Snake Bit's crew chief and door-gunner were onboard when Tatarski and Wall approached; they were ready to fly.

As critical as the situation was, however, it would have to wait; the day had dawned—as with the day before—with a thick fog severely restricting visibility around Tay Ninh. Soldiers often complain of the Army's hurry-up-and-wait mentality, but on this day, no one could fault the Army. Waiting on weather was the order of the day. Anxious to get the critical supplies to the ARVN soldiers in Cambodia, the guys made several attempts to fly throughout the morning—each attempt rebuffed by the lingering fog. By late morning, a small hole opened in the overcast, creating a brief respite; Tatarski and Wall took advantage of the opportunity and became one of the few ships to get airborne out of Tay Ninh. They immediately rendezvoused with two Cobra gunships and set a compass heading west to Cambodia.

The fog cleared before reaching the Cambodian border, but the weather was the least of their problems. The jungle canopy was thick, negating any possibility of making visual contact with the ARVN below, and without smoke, the ARVN were unable to mark their position.

Tatarski and Wall would have to utilize a little radio-direction-finding and home in on the ARVN's radio signals. Using their FM radio, they located the general area and began making passes to narrow the ARVN's position. Tatarski and Wall narrowed the ARVN's position on each pass. Each pass also revealed the severity of the situation. As the ARVN radio signal indicated they were close to their position, the NVA would open up with small arms fire; the ARVN and NVA positions were virtually one and the same. After establishing voice communications, it became obvious from the gunfire in the background that the ARVN were in an intense fire-fight. It was now time to call in the Cobra gunships to lay down suppressive fire on the enemy, but without smoke to mark the good-guys' position, the Cobra pilots would risk taking out their allies; their suppressive firepower would itself be suppressed by the lack of smoke.

With the ARVN below the jungle canopy, putting 2-4-0 on the ground was not possible. The canopy was so thick that even when Tatarski and Wall knew they were directly above the ARVN, they couldn't see the ground. They spotted a small opening in the upper part of the canopy, just above the ARVN, but it was barely large enough to hover part way to the ground; it had become a "hover-down and kick-out" mission. They would have to hover-down as close to the ground as possible and then literally kick their cargo out the side doors; the ARVN's new advisor would have to stay onboard and forgo the fight. Tatarski had flown these kinds of missions before and he knew that they could be hairy, scary, and sometimes downright deadly.

Even before coming to a hover, Snake Bit—"The Magnet"—began attracting intense automatic weapons fire from all sides. Tatarski and Wall were not deterred or intimidated by the green tracer rounds streaking past their windshield or the sound of hot lead hitting their ship. Snake Bit's crew chief and door gunner returned fire with their M-60 machine guns, directing their red tracers at the source of the enemy's green tracers.

After coming to a hover over the partial opening in the canopy, Tango began the hover-down. The hover-down was actually a four-man job; Tango and Wall were watching the trees to the front, left, and right while their door-gunner and crew chief were sending directions to move the tail left or right in order to clear the trees; all the while returning fire with their M-60s. It was a disquieting job requiring teamwork and meticulous coordination by all hands.

With eyeballs transfixed on tree branches seemingly inches away, green tracer rounds from the enemy's automatic weapons continued lighting the sky and hot lead continued impacting Snake Bit. In the midst of the chaos, Tatarski slumped over his cyclic stick and Snake Bit began to flounder. Wall fought against Tatarski's weight on his cyclic to regain control and yelled for his crew to grab Tango and pull him off the controls. Les Tatarski had obviously been hit by ground fire.

As Wall fought to regain control, Snake Bit's main rotor began chopping branches off the trees. It was time to get the hell out of there, if they could.

WO1 Larry Wall at the controls of a Huey
Photo Courtesy of Larry Wall

www.roy-mark.com/Pics_Fixin/Wall-1.jpeg

The crew chief and door-gunner left their M-60s for the more pressing task of pulling Tatarski off the controls. They came forward, tilted the pilot's seat back, and dragged Tango off the controls and into the back. With Snake Bit's two M-60s now silent, the emboldened enemy intensified their attack on the hovering Huey. With the sound of enemy lead hitting Snake Bit and green tracers streaking by, Wall slowly began to lift Snake Bit out of the trees.

In the back, the advisors began kicking supplies out the open doors as soon as they began taking ground fire. On the ground, smoke grenades, ammo, and other supplies rained down on the ARVN soldiers even as Snake Bit struggled to clear the trees. On the ground, the enemy was stunned to see what they thought was a sure kill slowly gain control and fly over the tree tops and out of their gun-sights.

As Wall regained control of Snake Bit and cleared the canopy, his focus turned to getting Tatarski to an aid station; doing so, however, was predicated on keeping his ship in the air. Snake Bit had been peppered with ground fire and was now showing the effects.

Wall left the firefight behind and headed for Vietnam and the nearest hospital. The safest altitude was at treetop level; at that level, any enemy below could put a bead on him ever so briefly. He knew, too, that the nearest aid station was at Quan Loi, just across the border. At his altitude, though, he couldn't home in on Quan Loi's radio signal, or for that matter even call ahead to advise the hospital of his casualty. Besides, dialing in the right frequencies on several different radios was out of the question; he had both hands full just keeping Snake Bit in the air. Knowing that his Cobra escorts would be above him at about two-thousand feet, and since they were on his radio frequency, he keyed his mike and asked them for a heading to Quan Loi. The Coba pilot roger'ed that and said he would notify the Quan Loi hospital of their pending arrival.

Wall pushed the air speed to VNE[28], which, since Snake Bit's doors had been removed, was only ninety-two miles per hour. Snake Bit resisted; she would have none of it and protested with severe vibrations, causing Wall to back off. He tried several times to increase the speed, but Snake Bit was adamant: take it easy or risk total destruction. Seventy miles per hour seemed to be the maximum speed Snake Bit would tolerate. Fortunately, Quan Loi was only ten minutes away, even at the reduced speed.

Inside Snake Bit, with vibrations threatening fiery doom into the jungle below, the ten minutes it took to reach Quan Loi seemed more like an hour. Once inside the Quan Loi perimeter, however, the feeling of relief was almost palpable. Wall sat Snake Bit down on the dedicated helipad next to the surgical hospital. Medics quickly removed Tatarski, put him on a gurney, and wheeled him into the emergency room.

Larry Wall hurried through his shutdown procedure and brought Snake Bit to an idle. Without waiting for the engine cool-down period, he jumped out and directed his crew chief to the co-pilot's seat with instructions to keep her idled and on the pad; the crew chief knew to protect against a sudden gust of wind blowing the idling Huey off the pad.

Wall hurried into the emergency room to check on his aircraft commander and friend. It happened so fast: the surgeon had opened Tatarski's chest and was standing with a dejected look on his face.

---

[28] VNE (Velocity Never to be Exceeded) on the UH-1H with doors removed was 80 Knots or about 92 miles per hour.

"It's over, there's nothing we could do for him" was all the doctor could say. He explained that an AK-47 bullet had entered the patient's chest on a downward trajectory and had destroyed the upper part of his heart.

Wall walked back to Snake Bit to break the news to his crew. A medic was there telling his crew chief to move the wounded Huey off the pad because another causality was expected soon. The crew chief of course wasn't a qualified pilot, so Wall took over and flew Snake Bit a short distance away. It was Snake Bit's last flight of the day; actually, it was her last *powered* flight of the day.

A crowd gathered around Snake Bit as Wall and his crew began examining their wounded Huey. It took a while, but they finally counted forty-eight bullet holes in "The Magnet," one of which told a grim story. Near the upper part of the pilot's door, on the left side where Tatarski had sat, a 7.62 mm AK-47 bullet had entered and hit a steel lug on the upper doorframe. The bullet then deflected downward, entering Les Tatarski's body next to the seam of his chicken plate.

A couple of other bullet strikes explained the severe vibrations experienced after the attack. Two bullets had hit the push-pull tubes connecting to the main rotor. The push-pull tubes are part of the rotor pitch-control mechanism—vital for maintaining control—and when damaged even slightly, can bring down a helicopter. It was obvious that Snake Bit would not fly again that day, and obvious, too, that Wall had done an amazing job in keeping her in the air at all.

Major Bailey, felt he owed his life to Larry Wall. He later said, "WO1 Wall's cool, uncommon courage and his decisive action under fire saved the lives of the rest of the crew and the passengers."

It had been a long, hard, and stressful day for the co-pilot, crew, and passengers of Huey 68-15240. Major Bailey and his lieutenant were worried about the fate of their ARVN comrades and immediately set about arranging to return to the fight. In the meantime, they could only hope that the supplies they had kicked out of Snake Bit over the fire-fight got to the good guys and not the bad.

Snake Bit and her surviving crew flew back to Tay Ninh late that afternoon; the soldiers were inside a giant CH-47 Chinook helicopter with Snake Bit—wounded but proud—strapped to the Chinook's underbelly.

Back in Tay Ninh, Charlie Company's commanding officer, Captain Roger Baker began the grim tasks required in the aftermath of the death of one of his soldiers. Arrangements were made for a memorial service. An officer would have to be assigned to escort Les Tatarski's body back to his home in Buffalo, New York. Captain Baker called for Tatarski's closest friend, WO1 Joe Schaefer, and asked if he would consent to taking on the responsibility of escort duty. Schaefer—like Tatarski—was a quiet, serious individual and was still shaken from the news of his friend's death. He asked for time to consider the request but returned the next day and told Captain Baker that Les had been his best friend; he couldn't say no. Les Tatarski left behind a wife of less than a year and a new baby he had never seen. Consoling the family would be the toughest part of Schaefer's escort duty.

Joe Schaefer was a short-timer, so after his escort duties, he was not required to report back to Captain Baker in Vietnam. They did meet again, though, many years later as civilians. At a Vietnam Helicopter Pilots Association[29] (VHPA) reunion, good times and sad times were reminisced. When Les Tatarski's death was brought up, Baker asked Schaefer about the escort duty. Schaefer paused and looked at Baker with faraway eyes. He finally said that it was the hardest thing he had ever done in his life and that it haunts him still.

In Tay Ninh, Vietnam, life—and the war—went on. Warrant Officer Leslie Miles Tatarski was posthumously awarded the Silver Star Medal for his actions on 12 June 1970. On 20 June, Warrant Officer Larry Wall was awarded the Distinguished Flying Cross (DFC). The DFC medal was pinned on Wall's uniform by Brigadier General Jonathan Burton, who was the Assistant Division Commander of 1st Cavalry Division.

---

[29] www.vhpa.org

Brigadier General Jonathan Burton, Assistant Division Commander, 1st Cavalry Div.
Awards the Distinguished Flying Cross to WO1 Larry Wall
In the Background, WO1 Steve Adams Assists the General in Awarding Medals
Tay Ninh, Republic of Vietnam, 20 June 1970

www.roy-mark.com/Pics_Fixin/Wall-2.jpg

Snake Bit was repaired and, with no fanfare, re-entered service as 68-15240; she was still "The Magnet" to her crew.

After a solid two months of combat, U.S. forces ended their participation in the Cambodian operation on 30 June 1970.

With WO1 Joe Schaefer escorting Tatarski's body back to New York, Charlie Company was losing two experienced aircraft commanders. The sudden void created a critical situation, but experience and talent were waiting in the wings.

Since their arrival in Vietnam in the spring of 1970, Larry Wall, Bob Bauer, and Mark Holtom had morphed from FNGs to fully competent Huey pilots. Their skills in aviation and tactics on combat missions in Vietnam and Cambodia impressed their aircraft commanders and their commanding officer. The trio was elevated from co-pilots to aircraft commanders; Charlie Company didn't miss a beat.

With the Cambodian Incursion now in their rearview mirror, the entire 229th Assault Helicopter Battalion received order to pack up and move. Charlie Company—call sign "North Flag"—was headed south.

5 BACK IN VIETNAM

After the Cambodian Incursion ended on 30 June 1970, the battalion received orders to move sixty miles to the southeast and setup in the U.S. base at Bien Hoa. (See map on page 20.)

Charlie Company's CO, Captain Roger Baker, began organizing the move to Ben Hoa; there was much to be done. The men of Charlie Company may have been anticipating conditions at their new home in Ben Hoa, but the CO's mind was elsewhere. Baker's tour in Vietnam had ended; upon Charlie Company's arrival in Ben Hoa, Baker would hand command of the company over to a battalion staff officer and board a "freedom bird" for stateside duty at Fort Stewart, Georgia.

Preparations for the move to Bien Hoa required that everyone pitch in with the mundane task of packing. In the company orderly room, files were packed into boxes, typewriters wrapped and packed, and larger items such as file cabinets and office furniture packed into shipping containers. The supply section tackled the massive job of preparing tons of supplies for shipment. The officers and men prepared their personal belongings for shipment as well. Charlie Company didn't have the luxury of moving at a leisurely pace; there was a war to fight and time was at a premium.

One of the last things to be packed—perhaps the most important in the minds of many of Charlie Company's officers—was the officer's club. The O Club was a wooden structure that the company had taken over from the ARVN a few years earlier.

The officers found that the club's interior became quite hot in the tropical heat and, as such, was not conducive to their leisure enjoyment. The structure was in need of insulation, but the Army wasn't about to ship insulation material halfway around the world—not knowingly anyway. The Army did ship tons upon tons of ordnance, among which was magnesium parachute flares that Charlie Company dropped by the dozens during night ground attacks. The flares were about two feet long and were packed in polystyrene foam. A resourceful GI, no longer content to drink cold beer in a hot club, observed that the polystyrene packing foam fit nicely between the studs of the walls and the ceiling joist. The "insulation" was put to good use.

In the Army tradition of "shit rolls down hill," the task of packing the O Club fell to the most junior of the officers. A group of nineteen to twenty-one-year-old warrant officers was charged not only with packing the contents of the club—case upon case of beer—but with returning the structure to its original condition.

With alcohol readily available, it was inevitable that some—better make that copious amounts of—beer was consumed. To lighten the mood further, WO1 Mark Holtom broke out his collection of music cassettes. The music and beer, combined with good friends working together created a party atmosphere.

After most of the club's contents were packed, the young warrant officers then set about—as per their orders—returning the structure to its original, uninsulated condition. As the polystyrene foam was pulled from the walls and a large pile began to accumulate, the guys began breaking them into pieces that were more manageable. Actually, more manageable pieces was secondary to the fun they were having karate chopping the errant foam. As time went on—and beer consumed—the karate moves became more and more elaborate and exaggerated. Japanese movie directors would have been impressed, if only they had been there and could observe through alcohol-impaired eyes.

Late in the day, Larry Wall did a 180-degree rotation culminating in a karate chop to what he expected to be a polystyrene enemy to his rear. His imaginary enemy, as it turned out, was Holtom's hardwood box containing his music tapes. The oak box gave no ground to the metacarpal bone in Wall's hand. Even with the anesthetic effects of the beer, it soon became painfully obvious to Wall that serious damage had been done to his hand.

At the aid station, x-rays confirmed that the metacarpal bone between Wall's wrist and little finger was broken. After keeping his hand on ice for a day, a plaster cast was put on his right arm from fingers to biceps. The tips of the fingers on his right hand was all that extended from the cast, and to make matters worse, his thumb was set almost perpendicular to his fingers.

With the cast restricting full mobility in his right hand, Wall would be unable to grip the cyclic stick and apply the precision input required for flight. WO1 Larry Wall, one of Charlie Company's newest aircraft commanders, was grounded for the six to eight week healing process.

Once Charlie Company settled into their new digs at Bien Hoa, they discovered that conditions were much improved. The Air Force also had an airfield at Bien Hoa, and Charlie Company personnel soon learned that the amenities at the Air Force Base were far superior to their own. At the Army base, troops sat outside on hard benches to watch movies projected onto chunks of plywood painted white hanging from the backside of the mess hall. It was no wonder then that the guys often trekked over to the Air Force Base where they could watch movies indoors in a proper theater. The Air Force also sported a Base Exchange that was modern, air conditioned, and well stocked. The Army's dull and sparingly appointed clubs seemed uninviting after just one visit to an Air Force club.

In a quirk of military rank structure, Air Force Senior Airman (Pay Grade E-4) were Non-Commissioned Officers (NCOs), but the Army's equivalent, Specialists Fourth Class and Corporal—although equal in pay grade—were not. The Army E-4s would often visit the Air Force base where they were cordially welcomed into the Air Force NCO Club.

229th Assault Helicopter Battalion base at Bien Hoa
Photo Courtesy of SP4 John Hubbs, C and B/229th Avn Bn 1971 – 1972
www.229thavbn.com

www.roy-mark.com/Pics_Fixin/229-Base.jpg

At Bien Hoa, the pace of missions slackened, and flying for the pilots of C/229th became routine, if flying in a war zone can ever be considered routine. Even so, the pilots were logging close to, and in some cases in excess of, the maximum hours allowed by the Army. The

Battalion's flight surgeon would routinely issue waivers to the 110 hours per month maximum; the war, it seems, had priority over protocol.

WO1 Larry Wall—his right arm still in a cast—spent his first couple of months at Bien Hoa doing endless, mundane ground assignments. When the cast was finally cut off, Wall was anxious to take to the skies. He was surprised though, at how weak his right hand had become during the idle months in the cast. His hand was not only weak, but also very painful when he tried to grip anything. It was a concern, but he was ready to fly and felt up to the challenge.

On his fist day in the cockpit since the battalion moved to Bien Hoa, Wall drew a mission with a FNG pilot. His FNG peter-pilot was a new arrival that would be flying his first mission in-country. It wasn't particularly a long day of flying; eight-hour days were routine. After eight hours though, Wall's already weak hand could hardly grip his cyclic-stick. His peter-pilot, being on his first mission, was of no help. Procedure called for FNG pilots to ride and observe for the first couple of days; Wall and his weak right hand were on their own. It was a relief when Wall was finally able to shut down at Bien Hoa; the hand needed a rest.

Rest for Wall's injured hand was not in the cards; upon landing, Wall's radio crackled to life, and a new mission assigned. Wall and his FNG peter-pilot were to fly a "sniffer" mission.

The mission called for Wall to fly with a "people sniffer" installed on his Huey. The people sniffers— officailly, "M3 personnel detectors"—could detect the telltale effluents of humans, such as the ammonia given off from sweat and urine. The sniffer consoles were mounted inside the cabin with long hoses snaking down to the skids with scoops to sample the air-flow for signs of humans below. For best results, sniffer pilots would fly at a very slow speed, just above the treetop.

In enemy held territory, it was a good way to pinpoint their positions under heavy foliage. The sniffers could detect even an enemy hiding in a cave; the ammonia rising through the vent holes was a dead giveaway.

WO1 Larry Wall tried to beg off the sniffer mission; after eight hours of flying, his hand was just too weak. Wartime reality—too many missions to fly with too few pilots—was of higher priority, so Wall set about in preparation for the sniffer mission. Before the mission, the Huey needed to be fueled, so Wall and his FNG peter-pilot cranked up the Huey for the short trip to the fueling pad. His FNG had—as per protocol—been observing all day; Wall decided to give his injured hand—and his FNG—a break and let his new peter-pilot fly the short distance to the fueling pad.

The short flight went well until the approach to the pad. The FNG brought the Huey in a little fast and then overcompensated with an exaggerated flare. His flare—raising the nose and lowering the tail for landing—was so exaggerated, that the tail boom dug into the dirt. The tail boom immediately broke off and the Huey rotated right causing the main rotor blades to dig into the ground as well. The Huey came to rest on its side, a total wreck.

No one was hurt in the accident, at least not physically. Wall's newly acquired aircraft commander status however, became the main casualty. As aircraft commander, protocol dictated that he not allow an FNG on the controls on his first day. Wall would now serve as the most experienced, well-respected peter-pilot in Charlie Company.

Tom "The Ogre" Agnew did not make the move to Bien Hoa; he finished his tour months before and returned to "the world." The Ogre's House, however, did make the move and was reconstituted at Bien Hoa.

Coincidentally, at Ben Hoa, Bob "Little Ogre" Bauer was billeted in The Ogre's House along with Holtom and six other warrant officers. The eight pilots of The Ogre's House became quite close, almost like brothers. In their after-hours, they joked around, shot the shit, played music, wrote letters, and drank beer.

Early on, The Ogre's House was occupied exclusively by warrant officers. Commissioned officer pilots were segregated into separate hooches. Later, as personnel came and went, and a few warrant officers received direct commissions, the hooches became less defined with a mixture of warrant and commissioned officers.

The Army's propensity to assign nomenclature to every item in its inventory down to toilet seats, created imaginative new words. The General Purpose "GP" vehicle became known simply as "Jeep," and many years later the "High-Mobility Multi-purpose Wheeled Vehicle," or "HMMWV," would be slurred into the word "Humvee." Similarly, commissioned officers, in good natured ribbing, referred to their "WO1" comrades as

"Wobbly Ones." The Wobbly Ones countered by referring to their commissioned counterpart as "RLO," short for "Real Live Officer."

Dan Tyler arrived in Vietnam in March 1970 as a "Wobbly" and later accepted a direct commission as second lieutenant. Rather than move to an "RLO Hooch," Dan remained in The Ogre's House; one "Wobbly Hooch" became desegregated.

Dan was a Nebraska farm boy that learned to fly while he was in high school. He left the farm for the University of Nebraska, but the lure of aviation was strong, so after one year he put his education on hold and joined the Army to fly helicopters. After becoming an aircraft commander, Dan adopted the personal call sign "Gentleman Dan."

Chief Warrant Officer 2 (CWO2) Jack McCormick was another resident of The Ogre's House and hooch mate of Bauer and Holtom at Bien Hoa. Jack was a Southern boy from Memphis, Tennessee. He became interested in aviation at an early age and, while still a teen, joined his local Civil Air Patrol. His activities in the C.A.P. only intensified his desire to learn to fly. After graduating high school, Jack met a buddy's older brother who was a pilot for Eastern Airlines[30]. That encounter sparked a desire, and aviation became Jack's intended vocation. Jack began quizzing his friend's brother about how best to pursue his dream. One route discussed to becoming a professional pilot was military flight training, so when

---

[30] Eastern Airlines went out of business in 1991. Their last flight was on 19 January 1991.

the not-unanticipated draft notice arrived, Jack opted to join the Army and learn to fly helicopters.

Steve Adams lived in the next hooch over, or it should be said that he slept there since he spent much of his free time visiting with his buddies in The Ogre's House. Adams was from Johnson County in Eastern Kentucky and spoke with a distinct Southern accent, which prompted good-natured kidding from the other pilots. The nearest place to Adam's home was a small crossroads community called Redbush. When Adams first arrived in Vietnam and was asked where he was from, he replied in his country drawl, "Redbush, Kentucky." It was inevitable then that Adams' personal call sign became "Redbush."

Before leaving Tay Ninh, Bob Bauer and Mark Holtom were elevated to aircraft commanders and, as such, were required to have a personal radio call sign when flying. Bauer's call sign was a slam-dunk: he had been "Little Ogre" since soon after his arrival in the company. Holtom's call sign became "Hokus Pokus."

Within every group of guys, one will usually emerge as the jokester, the guy with the wit and ability to lighten the mood. Bob "Little Ogre" Bauer fit that bill. His outgoing personality and joviality helped all in the hooch deal with the seriousness and stress of war. It was usually in The Ogre's House that the pilots gathered for after-hours bull sessions.

Left to Right: Larry Wall, Bob "Little Ogre" Bauer
and Mark "Hokus Pokus" Holtom
In "The Ogre's House" at Tay Ninh
Notice "The Ogre's House" sign in the background
Photo Courtesy of Greg Holtom

www.roy-mark.com/Pics_Fixin/Wall_Bauer_Holtom.jpg

6 EVE OF DESTRUCTION

As night fell on Friday, 25 September, the guys gathered as usual in The Ogre's House. Most of the guys had flown that day, and most were scheduled to fly the next. The tensions of war were eased, and moods lightened as jokes were told and beer flowed.

With Ogre's House filled with music and beer readily available, the guys interspersed routine activities into a party atmosphere. Little Ogre fixed a nice birthday card for his grandmother that he would send the next day. Then, considering the others as brothers, asked them to write personal greetings on the card—greetings to a grandmother they had never met. The greetings and comments written were light-hearted and jovial; it was great fun.

Mark "Hokus Pokus" Holtom was the music-meister of the bunch and always supplied music from his vast collection. As Friday night turned into early Saturday morning, Mark pulled out his copy of,

"I-Feel-Like-I'm-Fixin'-to-Die-Rag" by Country Joe and the Fish. The recording, from the Woodstock Album, was a favorite in The Ogre's House, and they all relished singing in unison.

And it's one, two, three,
What are we fighting for?
Don't ask me, I don't give a damn,
Next stop is Vietnam;
And it's five, six, seven,
Open up the pearly gates,
Well there ain't no time to wonder why,
Whoopee! we're all gonna die.

Words and lyrics by Joe McDonald
© 1965 Alkatraz Corner Music Co.BMI
renewed 1993

By 2:30 on Saturday morning, the party fizzled, and the guys all crashed for some much needed, albeit abbreviated, sleep.

While they were sleeping off the beers, the tactics for the next day's missions were worked out at the brigade level. By early morning, their orders were passed down to Charlie Company. When the staff at Charlie Company received their orders, they in turn began allocating crews to aircraft and preparing mission sheets for each aircraft commander.

About 45 minutes before Saturday's mission was to begin, the pilots in Ogre's House were roused from their sleep. After long cold showers, aircraft commanders picked up a copy of the mission sheet from TOC. They then joined the rest of the crews in the mess hall for bacon and greasy eggs.

7 SKY PILOT

Saturday's mission called for a five-ship gaggle to fly the short distance to FSB Green. At Green, they would pick up soldiers of the 1st Brigade, 7th Rifle Company for transport to Landing Zones in the field. "Gentleman Dan" Tyler would be the Air Mission Commander on the day's mission with Larry Wall as his peter-pilot.

After chow, Peter-Pilots Francis Sullivan and Warren Lawson made their way to the flight line for routine pre-flight inspections of their helicopters. "Sully" would be flying with AC Mark "Hokus Pokus" Holtom. Hokus and Sully's Huey that day would be tail number 68-15648, a ship with an interesting past.

Huey 6-4-8 was manufactured by Bell Helicopter Company in Fort Worth, Texas. After coming off the assembly line in 1968, the Army shipped 6-4-8 to Vietnam, arriving in Charlie Company in mid-1969. The new Huey's first crew chief was a short-timer, soon to be charged with breaking in his replacement, SP4 David

Holte. When 6-4-8 began flying missions, as with all Hueys in a combat zone, it was inevitable that it would sometimes receive ground fire. With 6-4-8, it seemed that anytime FNG passengers were onboard, taking ground fire was inevitable. Huey 6-4-8 seemed to have an affinity for busting FNG cherries.

Later when the Battalion commander authorized his Huey crews to name and paint nose art on their ships, Crew Chief Holte and his door-gunner kicked around ideas for a name. It wasn't much of a debate; 6-4-8 seemed to have named itself: "Cherry Buster." David Holte designed and adorned 6-4-8 with nose art depicting two bleeding red cherries.

In 1969, Huey 6-4-8 was assigned to Captain Roger Baker. When he saw the nose art depicting two bleeding red cherries and the name "Cherry Buster," Baker immediately instructed his crew chief, David Holte to change the name to "Easy Rider." The road movie by the same name, starring Peter Fonda, was very popular at the time. Holte then explained that 6-4-8 was so named because of the propensity for FNGs to receive their baptism of fire in that ship. Then, according to Captain Baker, SP4 Holte "respectfully informed" him that changing the name of an aircraft was bad luck; 6-4-8 remained "Cherry Buster." The two cherries however had to go, so Baker and Holte came up with a new concept. Baker, being an accomplished artist, painted new art onto 6-4-8's nose. Inspired by the cartoon character Mighty Mouse, Cherry Buster's new art depicted a character holding a sword with "Cherry Buster" across his muscular chest. Captain Baker, who later became commanding officer of Charlie Company, had transferred out of the company by the time Hokus and Sully manned Cherry Buster on that Saturday morning.

Cherry Buster's Second Nose Art
Painted by Captain Roger Baker
Photo Courtesy of Roger Baker

www.roy-mark.com/Pics_Fixin/Cherry-Buster.jpg

Lawson did his pre-flight inspection on 68-16123, dubbed "Thumpy 1." (See photo on page 34.) He would be flying with AC Bob "Little Ogre" Bauer. Larry Wall and the other two peter-pilots of the mission performed their pre-flights as well.

During pre-flight inspections by the peter-pilots, aircraft commanders made their way to TOC to check for any last minute changes to the mission. They then joined their crews on the flight line.

Bob "Little Ogre" Bauer joined his peter-pilot, "Wild Bill" Lawson in Thumpy 1. Thumpy 1's crew chief, Doug Woodland, and Door-Gunner Robert Painter were busy mounting their M-60 machine guns.

Twenty-year-old SP4 Bobby Painter was from New Jersey, but three years before joining the Army, he and his family moved to Indian Head, Maryland. Bobby Painter came from a large family; he had four younger brothers and four younger sisters. Bobby loved all things mechanical and had a knack for fixing them when they went wrong. Back in Indian Head, he would spend hours fixing up his old VW Bug and would always make time for his younger brothers when they showed up to help. Bobby even allowed his youngest brother, four-year-old Andrew, to "help" fix his blue bug and enjoyed taking him for a joy-ride afterwards. By the time Bobby joined the Army, he was a skilled mechanic, having studied auto mechanics and graduating from Lincoln Technical Institute. Painter was still considered a "new guy," in-country just fifty-six days, but that was more than enough days to know he didn't much like the place.

At 19, SP4 Woodland was younger than Painter, but as Thumpy 1's crew chief was his senior and had been in Vietnam four months. Doug Woodland was from

Scottsdale, Arizona, and had celebrated his 19th birthday earlier that month.

A short distance from Thumpy 1, Mark Holtom joined his crew in Cherry Buster where Peter-Pilot Francis Sullivan was setting up to perform a radio check. Cherry Buster had been designated by Brigade as "White One" for the day's mission, so Sully checked each of his radios by calling another ship, "Yellow Two, Yellow Two (Thumpy 1) this is White One, radio check, over." It was not until each radio of all of the helicopters received a response of, "loud and clear" that the mission was good to go.

Cherry Buster's co-pilot, Lieutenant Francis Sullivan, was from East Hartford Connecticut and was older than most of Charlie Company's pilots. With his 28th birthday less than a month away, back in the States, his wife was probably already shopping for a small gift to send her new husband. Francis had been married about a year and had a new son. Sully had more time in the Army—two years, eight months—than most of the other guys. Having arrived in-country a little less than two months earlier, however, he was still considered a new guy.

Sullivan, a quiet-spoken but athletic and imposing figure, had played baseball and basketball in high school and at the University of Bridgeport. He even studied for his masters in physical education for a while at the University of Iowa.

Cherry Buster's door-gunner, SP4 Ernest Laidler, and Crew Chief Donald Hall were mounting their M-60s and preparing for the mission. Laidler was from Abington, Massachusetts, just south of Boston. The twenty-year-old door-gunner had arrived just the prior month; he was still considered a new guy.

SP4 Donald Hall, Cherry Buster's crew chief, was no new guy. After eight and a half months in-country, Hall was beginning to look forward to his "DEROS," Army speak for "Date of Expected Return from Overseas," and soldier speak for "return to the world." His plans no doubt were to return to his family in Millington, Michigan, a small town about 20 miles northeast of Flint. Hall had seen a lot in Vietnam. After his arrival in January, Hall began work as a cook; he was quickly tagged with the nickname "Spoon." Spoon Hall didn't much like his nickname but resented being "referred to as "REMF" (Rear Echelon Mother Fucker). In fact, Spoon hated it so much that he began bugging the First Sergeant for a transfer to a flight platoon. The First Sergeant finally relented, and Don "Spoon" Hall shed his mess hall apron to become a door-gunner, and a damn good one. He soon took over as crew chief, but, to the guys of Charlie Company, Don Hall was still "Spoon" Hall.

Donald "Spoon" Hall
Cooking Hamburgers in Charlie Company Mess Hall
Photo Compliments of John "PJ" Pecha

www.roy-mark.com/Pics_Fixin/Hall_Donald.jpg

As a crew chief, Spoon Hall began taking a large serving spoon from the mess hall with him on missions. He would hang his spoon on a pole near his crew chief's position. All crew chiefs stored some of the tools of their trade on the pole, which included smoke grenades. The smoke grenades came in white, red, green, and yellow, and to facilitate fast identification, the Army painted colored stripes on the body of the grenades. The brightly colored grenades hanging on the pole looked to some like Christmas bulbs, so of course the pole became known as a Christmas tree.

Hall's spoon hanging on his Christmas tree was not only his trademark but a functional tool as well. Passengers, unlike the Huey's crewmembers, were not on the intercom system, so in the noisy environment of the Huey, if Hall found it necessary to communicate with one of his passengers, he first had to get their attention. To do so, Don "Spoon" Hall would retrieve his trusty spoon from the Christmas tree and whoop the grunt atop his steel pot[31]. It never failed to arouse attention, and a few smiles. After becoming an experienced crew chief, Don was sometimes called upon to train a new crewmember. They, too, were known to be "spooned" if not performing to Spoon Hall's standards.

The official barrier between officers and enlisted men would begin to evaporate somewhat on the flight-line. In the air, the mutual respect between pilots and crews sometimes manifested itself in ways that to outsiders would seem strange. Pilots would occasionally catch the crews off guard with unexpected flight maneuvers. A pilot might initiate a steep climb culminating in a stall. The stall and subsequent nose-down dive toward the earth below was more thrilling than any amusement park ride and guaranteed to jump-start the flow of adrenalin. When the pilots erupted in uncontrolled laughter, the crew chief was apt to return the favor with a whack across the back of the pilot's helmet with a large screwdriver. Don Hall's pilot, of course, would get

---

[31] Army slang for helmet

"spooned" to renewed laughter. It was great fun and ultimate signs of respect on the part of officers and enlisted men working together in harrowing and dangerous times.

8 RIDE OF THE VALKYRIES

After all the Hueys of the gaggle had completed their radio checks, Air Mission Commander Dan Tyler conferred with his second-in-command, "Little Ogre" Bauer. Dan told Ogre that he would fly ahead to reconnoiter the LZs and then confer with the Task Force Commander at FSB Green. He then instructed Bauer to follow with the other three ships in thirty minutes.

Shortly after Tyler's departure from Bien Hoa, he encountered a solid cloudbank. From about five-hundred feet above ground level, the clouds were solid up to about 3,500 feet.

The solid clouds persisted out to about 15 miles from FSB Green where the skies cleared and Green was virtually in the clear.

Dan "Gentleman Dan" Tyler
In Cambodia, 1970
Photo Courtesy of Daniel E. Tyler

www.roy-mark.com/Pics_Fixin/Tyler_Dan.jpg

"Gentleman Dan" then radioed back to "Little Ogre" instructions to bring the flight out "over the top" at four thousand feet.

The rest of the flight left Bien Hoa and climbed to four thousand feet into clear skies. They formed up into a diamond formation led by "Little Ogre" in Thumpy 1. As was the custom with Charlie Company pilots, their formation was tight. They prided themselves on their tight formations with separation between ships of just two rotor blades, or about ninety-six feet. On today's flight, everyone behind Thumpy 1 would be close enough behind the ship ahead to feel the exhaust heat and smell the burned JP-4[32] jet fuel of the ship ahead. "Hokus Pokus" in Cherry Buster was in the left echelon position with Steve "Redbush" Adams at right echelon. At the rear of the diamond—the "tail-end-Charlie" position—was Captain Bob Barnaba. Barnaba was the unit's instructor pilot. With Barnaba was a new guy as his peter-pilot.

After reaching altitude, Bauer instructed the flight to begin their Daily Engine Record Check, referred to simply as the "DER." The first step of the DER check required the pilots to set their altimeter to the standard 29.92 inches of mercury. With all altimeters in sync, the pilots then recorded readings such as RPM, torque, airspeed, temperatures, and pressures.

The first order of business before beginning the DER was to increase the separation between aircraft. During normal formation flying, they maintained a separation of about ninety-six feet. To perform their DERs, the Hueys extended their separation to 240 feet, or about five rotor disks.

Standard procedure called for the aircraft commanders to perform the DER with their peter-pilot at the controls. The peter-pilot, crew chief, and door-gunner were responsible for keeping a lookout for hazards, particularly other aircraft in the formation.

---

[32] "JP" is the abbreviation of "Jet Propellant." JP-4 Jet Fuel is a 50/50 mixture of kerosene and gasoline.

Upon completion of the DER, pilots would then perform a closing maneuver to regain normal separation.

Having finished the DER, Cherry Buster began the closing maneuver. Air speed was increased ever so slightly, and they began maneuvering to their right. The distance began to close between Thumpy 1 and Cherry Buster.

Off to Cherry Buster's right, in the right echelon position, Steve "Redbush" Adams was finishing his DER. After stowing his maintenance book, he looked up and witnessed a violent mid-air collision. Adams would later say it looked like Thumpy 1 had slowed a little and that Cherry Buster may have been a little fast during the closing maneuver.

Cherry Buster's main rotor impacted the tail boom of Thumpy 1, and all hell broke loose.

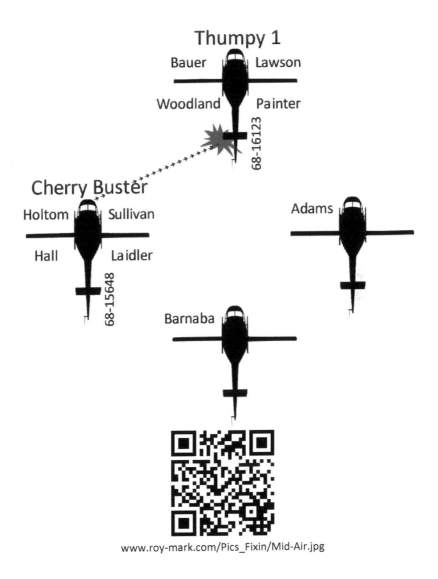

www.roy-mark.com/Pics_Fixin/Mid-Air.jpg

After the initial impact, Thumpy 1's main rotor cut into the cockpit of Cherry Buster and separated. Thumpy 1 rolled right and fell into the cloud layer; Cherry Buster went into a steep dive into the cloud. One body was seen falling clear of the carnage before they entered the cloud, but with so much flying debris from the collision it was not known who it was or even from which aircraft it came.

An instant after the carnage began, aircraft and ground stations for miles around heard a voice come on the radio and say, "Gooood Morning Vietnam, we've just had a mid-air collision." The voice did not identify itself, but of the guys that heard it and knew Bob Bauer, all knew that last "Gooood Morning..." came from "The Ogre." Dan Tyler would later say, "It was not a case of Bauer raising the alarm and hoping for assistance. Ogre had obviously resigned himself that it was over for him and he was cracking one last joke while he still could."

Steve Adams and Bob Barnaba, in the two remaining Hueys of the flight, began circling above the cloud cover and soon saw two distinct plums of black smoke rising through the white cloud. Adams radioed the news back to Bien Hoa and FSB Green.

Dan Tyler had just arrived at Green from his reconnaissance of the LZs when the news hit. He immediately got on the radio to Adams and learned it was Hokus and Little Ogre. Adams described seeing Cherry Buster and Thumpy 1 descending in uncontrolled flight into the cloud cover. He gave their position as near FSB Garry Owen[33,34] and an abandoned Vietnamese village called Rang Rang.

---

[33] FSB Gary Owen was located in War Zone D, III Corps, Long Khanh Provence, Republic of Vietnam.

[34] FSB Garry Owen was named after the Irish Air (Tune) "Garryowen" which was adopted as the march of the 7th Cavalry Regiment in 1867. It was said to be a favorite of General George Armstrong Custer and, according to legend, was the last tune played before the Battle of the Little Big Horn.

At altitude, the eyewitnesses had no doubt about the fatal outcome of such a violent mid-air collision. On the ground, feelings of hope overcame trepidation.

Dan Tyler immediately blasted off from FSB Green on a low-level search and rescue mission. Knowing that the gaggle would have flown from Ben Hoa on a north compass heading directly to Green, Tyler knew, too, that his best shot was to fly south on the compass reciprocal.

The overcast was still solid at five-hundred feet, and with a light mist further obscuring visibility, search conditions were not ideal. After flying about five minutes or so, his heart sank as he saw the unmistakable tell-tale signs of tragedy. From over the horizon rose two distinct columns of black smoke. It was gut wrenching; he knew in his heart that those columns of smoke rising to the heavens represented the lives of eight of his friends and colleagues.

Though understandably shaken, Adams and Barnaba maintained their professionalism. After Adams radioed the news to Tyler and battalion headquarters, he and Barnaba continued circling overhead. Barnaba finally found a hole in the clouds and spiraled down to join the search.

Jack McCormick, in Huey 7-5-4, which was nicknamed "the lil Texan[35]," was flying a different mission that day. On the ground at FSB Garry Owen, Jack heard the news on the lil Texan's radio and immediately set out on a search for his downed friends.

---

[35] "the lil Texan" was named after the former crew chief.

Actually, Jack didn't know for whom he was searching. He knew all of the guys on that mission, but he didn't know which of his friends had been involved in the mid-air.

As Tyler approached the two columns of smoke, he saw that they were about two hundred yards apart. He approached the first site and began to hover just above the small clearing in the jungle created by the impacting Huey. The fuselage was on its right side, totally engulfed in flames. The Huey's nearly full fuel cells were feeding the flames, exacerbated by the magnesium components used in Army helicopters[36]. Hoping against all hope for survivors, Tyler and his crew scanned the surrounding jungle. There was no sign of life outside and no possibility inside the intense flames. With the small clearing made by the impacting Huey engulfed in flames and no other clearing nearby big enough to land, there was nothing more Tyler could do there.

At the second crash site the scene was much the same except the main rotor blades were nowhere in sight. Looking for a place to land, Tyler saw several small openings in the canopy nearby. They looked even smaller as his crew chief and door-gunner tried to guide him down through the thick canopy. It was a gallant effort but each opening was just too small; they could get to about 60 feet above the ground, and no more.

Jack McCormick joined the search near Rang Rang. Flying between the ground fog, which was still clinging

---

[36] The magnesium components of the Huey would have begun to burn at five-hundred degrees Celsius (932° F) and then burned at three-thousand one-hundred degrees Celsius (5,600° F).

to the treetops and the low cloud cover made the search tedious at best. It wasn't long, however, before he saw it: black smoke mixed with the mist and fog rising from the forest canopy. It was an eerie scene. McCormick and his crew couldn't identify the Huey, in fact there was no helicopter to identify; what remained was the smoldering black outline of a Huey. The clearing was too small to land, so McCormick pinpointed the location and called for a search team.

For the remainder of that earth-shattering day, Charlie Company pilots and crews flew their missions. Ground crews performed their duties, cooks prepared meals, and the mail was delivered. On the surface, everything seemed the same, yet it would never be the same.

9 REMEMBER THE HEROES

Amemorial service for the fallen pilots and crews of the mid-air collision was held in the Charlie Company mess hall at Bien Hoa on 1 October 1970. The battalion Chaplin officiated with eulogies given by Second Lieutenant Dan Tyler and Sergeant First Class Frederick F. McAfee. Tyler, the commander of the fateful mission, eulogized the four aviators; his words have survived the decades:

> *According to a time-honored tradition we have gathered here in a memorial tribute to eight individuals who were lost to us through an inexplicable tragedy. Of all, it can be said that they were fine soldiers or officers, professionals who courageously faced every difficult task in this oft disheartening conflict and relentlessly strove to accomplish their mission. It is ironic that the tragedy which cost their lives*

was not more directly related to the combat environment they all knew.

Our country has indeed lost the services of eight very capable and very dedicated soldiers. But those of us who knew them best by living with them, working and flying alongside them, and enjoying with them the limited amount of relaxation time we were allowed, knew them as much more than the outstanding soldiers and officers they were. We knew them each as warm, friendly, and colorful individuals, persons who somehow added something, something intangible yet invaluable, to the lives of all those privileged enough to make their acquaintance. As the shock of their untimely death passes we who knew them as brothers in a tightly knit aviation fraternity come to realize the countless memories we will have of these eight, great guys. Those of us who knew them would like to share with those who weren't so fortunate some of the reasons these eight men stand so tall in our memories.

Of Warren Stephen Lawson, (22 Oct. 1947 – 26 Sept. 1970) Tyler said:

First Lieutenant Warren S Lawson came to Charlie Company in late July. He was a big, easy-going guy with a gentle, southern drawl. He seemed to fit in naturally with the rest of the guys, he had a ready smile, and he was quick with words of encouragement to whoever needed them. When the business at hand was serious, no one was more serious. But when the mood changed he was the first to laugh. Somewhere along the line somebody nicknamed him "Wild Bill" and the name stuck. As a section leader he showed a keen sense of responsibility and as a pilot he was an eager student of combat aviation. "Wild Bill" Lawson was an all-right guy.

Dan Tyler then memorialized Francis Jordan Sullivan (4 Nov. 1942 – 26 Sept. 1970):

First Lieutenant Francis J Sullivan arrived in Charlie Company in early August. He was sort of a quiet type of guy but once you got to know him, you were impressed by his friendliness and also by his keen perception. "Sully" learned fast and showed signs of someday becoming an outstanding aircraft commander. Not too many people knew the quiet New Englander well, but those who did, knew him as a warm and understanding friend.

Speaking of Robert Ernest Bauer (10 Mar. 1947 – 26 Sept. 1970) Tyler said:

Warrant Officer Robert E Bauer was assigned to this unit in the middle of last April. The "old guys" of North Flag nicknamed Bob "Little Ogre", after another member of the company who'd DEROS's way back when. When we invaded Cambodia in May and the stepped-up operations taxed our minds and bodies, Ogre always seemed to come through with the badly needed laughs. Though he saw some of the thickest action of the campaign, he somehow never lost his cherry – or his sense of humor. He made his name a kind of a legend and wherever he went people gathered around to hear "The Gospel According to Ogre". His wisecracks lightened the load we carried and his quips about the irony of war seemed to keep everything in perspective. Whenever we gathered for a few drinks and a few songs Little Ogre was there, leading the toasts and leading the songs. He knew well the bitterness of war and he kept it from getting any of us down. It's hard to believe his glowing smile is gone, for his gruff but hearty laughter still echoes loud and clear in our memories. Little Ogre was truly an unforgettable character.

Finally, memorializing Mark Richard Holtom (26 Mar. 1949 – 26 Sept. 1970) Second Lieutenant Dan "Gentleman Dan" Tyler said:

> *Warrant Officer Mark R Holtom arrived in Charlie Company in early April. Unlike the Ogre, Mark lost his cherry within a few weeks – but he never lost his cool. Before Hokus had been here three months he'd been shot up, shot down, and everything but blown away. But he still went out there, every day, never asking for slack, never taking any slack; his only request that he be left to his music when the missions for the day were complete. Hokus was a music nut – it didn't make any difference what kind of music it was. He liked some kinds better than others but he could derive pleasure from any music. He used to say he didn't care what anybody made him do or where he had to go, as long as he had his music. Yeah, Hokus was a real music nut, the greatest music nut we ever knew.*

Sergeant First Class McAfee then delivered the eulogy of the four lost enlisted men. McAfee undoubtedly spoke of courage, bravery, and the lost dreams and aspirations of four dedicated soldiers. Unfortunately, the words spoken on that sad day have not survived; however, the memory of the four will not die.

Ernest Hammond Laidler, Specialist Fourth Class, 022409650 (1 April 1950 – 26 September 1970). Ernest had been in Vietnam just 31 days and with his platoon only about three weeks. The guys of his platoon that gathered with Charlie Company for the memorial hardly knew Ernest Laidler. Most of the other members of Charlie Company probably searched their memory trying to place a face with the name. Ernest was from Abington, Massachusetts, a fact his new platoon mates may not have even known, although they probably would have guessed as much from his New England accent. Laidler may have been a new guy, but there was too much respect for his sacrifice to mention, or even think of him as a "FNG" on that day. Ernest Hammond Laidler was twenty years, five months, and twenty-five days old when he died.

Donald Allen Hall, Jr., Specialist Fourth Class, 362541120 (13 July 1949 – 26 September 1970). Donald Hall, the cook, turned door-gunner, turned crew chief was well known and well liked throughout Charlie Company. Don had been in-country eight and a half months and, although not yet considered a short-timer, he probably was already counting the months if not days before his return to the world. Don Hall was a dedicated soldier; he volunteered to exchange his relatively safe job as a cook for flight duty as a door-gunner. His performance was exemplary, and he was soon elevated to crew chief. Don Hall was a small-town boy from Millington, Michigan. His family would be devastated by the news of his death but could be proud of Don's passion and service to his country. Charlie Company was indeed honored to have known and served with Don "Spoon" Hall. Donald Allen Hall, Jr. was 21 years, 2 months, and 13 days old when he died. Specialist 4 Donald Hall was posthumously promoted to Sergeant E-5.

Robert Albert Painter, Jr., Specialist Fourth Class, 151422013 (1 November 1949 – 26 September 1970). Bob Painter had been in-country less than two months. In that short time, he had become proficient in his job as a door-gunner. At the memorial service, it was said that Bob was from Indian Head, Maryland, but anyone who knew him knew that he had lived there only a short time before entering the Army; he was a product of New Jersey. Bob Painter's parents, his four brothers, and four sisters would soon mourn his death as his Charlie Company brothers were now honoring his memory and service. Robert Albert Painter, Jr. was twenty years, ten months, and twenty-five days old at the time of this death.

Douglas Mead Woodland, Specialist Fourth Class, 526925663 (6 September 1951 – 26 September 1970). Doug Woodland had been in-country for four months and was a dedicated and proficient crew chief. He was respected and depended on by the pilots with whom he flew. Doug Woodland had celebrated his nineteenth birthday just twenty days before his tragic death. In fact, he was the youngest soldier to be memorialized on that sad day. Doug was from Scottsdale, Arizona. The guys attending the memorial service didn't know it, but Specialist 4 Douglas Woodland would be promoted posthumously to Sergeant E-5.

In Vietnam, the Army memorialized and honored the fallen, began their investigation, and prepared to send remains to grieving families. Back in the States, the difficult task of notification began.

A birthday card arrived in Pearl River, New York, with perfect timing; it was 29 September and the 86th birthday of Bob Bauer's grandmother. The family gathered around as the birthday wishes and silly comments were read. The card, signed by Bob and the guys of "The Ogre's House" brought great joy to the entire family—a joy derived from a silly birthday card to be treasured forever. Three hours after reading the birthday wishes, Army officers from nearby West Point Military Academy arrived and shattered the festive mood with the terrible news.

Two uniformed soldiers approached the home of Shirlie Holtom in Lakewood, California. Shirlie, the single mother of Mark and his two younger brothers was working, leaving her two youngest sons home alone. The soldiers did not identify themselves as "Causality Notification Officers"; they just asked the boys when their mother would be home. Foreboding gripped Mark's brothers, so they called an aunt, Shirlie's sister, to come to the house to be with their mother when the officers returned.

In Connecticut, Army officers arrived at Francis Sullivan's Manchester home. The news was devastating to his wife. In her grief, she then had to contemplate explaining to her young son, once he was old enough to understand, what happened to the father he would not remember.

In Scottsdale, Arizona, Doug Woodland's wife Vikki learned of the death of her husband, the father of their son, the father he had never seen.

In Millington, Michigan, the parents of Donald Allen Hall, Jr. were told of the death of their twenty-one-year-old son near a place called Rang Rang.

The visits by Army officers fulfilling their grim duties continued; in Milton, Florida, they made the dreaded visit to Warren Lawson's wife.

On the East Coast, the parents of Door-Gunners Ernest Laidler and Robert Painter were told of their sons' death. The Painter Family in Indian Head, Maryland, and the Laidler's in Abington, Massachusetts, each received the solemn visitors and began their grieving.

The grieving by the family and friends of the eight warriors was immediate and intense. The public, too, often showed support with acts of kindness and compassion. On 3 October, in Ellinwood Kansas, the mayor directed that all flags in the city would be flown at half-mast in Mark Holtom's honor. In East Hartford, Connecticut, the Chamber of Commerce honored the memory of Francis Sullivan by planting a mountain ash tree on the Main Street esplanade.

Bob "Little Ogre" Bauer was a prolific letter writer; he wrote his parents every day. He wrote often about his friendship with Mark Holtom and Larry Wall. The trio had been together since flight school at Fort Wolters, and their bond had only strengthened since their introduction into combat. Bauer also wrote letters to Mark's mother and to Larry's girlfriend, Nancy Shahan. Nancy often kidded Larry that Bob wrote her more often than he did, and she'd never even met Bob.

When the Army contacted the Bauer's asking if there was anyone special they would like to escort their son's remains back to New York, they didn't hesitate. They requested either of their son's best friends, Larry Wall or Mark Holtom. Shirlie Holtom, Mark's mother, requested that either of Mark' best friends, Larry Wall or Bob Bauer escort her son's remains back to California. The sad irony had to be explained to the grieving parents that one of their sons' best friends had died in the same accident.

Larry Wall had a tough decision to make; his two best friends' parents were requesting he honor their sons by escorting their remains to their final resting place. Ultimately, since he and Mark were both Southern California natives, Wall decided to escort Mark Holtom's body back to Lakewood, California where Mrs. Holtom lived.

Once Wall made his decision, he was told to attend an Army escort briefing where he would be briefed on his duties from the time he departed the preparing mortuary until his return to Vietnam. His mission as an escort, it was explained, was to ensure that WO1 Mark Richard Holtom's remains were safeguarded and properly moved from the time of release from the preparing mortuary until delivery to the receiving funeral home. The importance of the assignment was emphasized; he was instructed to maintain the highest standards of conduct and courtesy, including neatness of appearance and sobriety. Wall was told not to discuss the purpose of his travel with anyone other than the carrier's agents and representatives. Furthermore, it was emphasized that he was not to discuss with anyone rumors, speculation, or the circumstances of the incident surrounding the death of WO1 Mark Holtom.

The escort briefing went into the details of transporting the remains. Mark Holtom was to travel feet first from one point to another. The only exception would be during transport by aircraft when the head of the casket must be towards the nose of the aircraft. It was explained that this was done that way to prevent damage to the remains during takeoff and landing. Wall was to drape the interment flag on the casket with the stars over the left shoulder of the remains.

Wall began his grim and sad duty at Tay Ninh's mortuary. He escorted his friend onto a C-130 cargo plane for a flight to Ben Hoa. From Ben Hoa, he boarded a commercial chartered flight to Travis Air Force Base in Northern California. At Travis, Wall ensured that Mark's remains were transferred properly to another C-130 for a flight to Long Beach. A hearse met him at Long Beach for transportation to the mortuary. Mark was to be laid to rest at Forest Lawn Memorial Park in Long Beach.

Larry Wall then went to meet with Mrs. Holtom in Lakewood. He performed his official duties, but Mark was his friend, and this was a personal mission, too. He tried to comfort a grieving mother. She cried, and he cried; it was a very emotional.

At the graveside service on 7 October 1970, a twenty-one-gun salute was performed by soldiers from a local post. The soldiers removed The Stars and Stripes from the casket and ceremoniously folded it thirteen times into the traditional tri-cornered shape. Thirteen folds, each with a significance. According to tradition, the first fold of the flag is a symbol of life, the second fold the symbol of belief in eternal life, and the third fold is made in honor and remembrance of the veterans departing our ranks who gave a portion of their lives for the defense of our country to attain peace throughout the world. And so it went until the thirteenth fold created the tri-cornered shape.

WO1 Larry Wall was then to present the flag to Mark's mother. The emotions of the moment caught up with him; tears began to flow, and his body refused his commands. To salvage the ceremony, Wall asked one of the honor guard soldiers to present the flag to Mrs. Holtom.

Before returning to Vietnam, Wall took the opportunity to visit with his parents and, of course, his girlfriend, Nancy Shahan. Larry and Nancy decided they would get married. WO1 Larry Wall returned to Vietnam a married man.

Meanwhile, the war in Vietnam continued and the bitter fruits of that conflict continued to be returned to loved ones in flag-draped boxes. The U. S. government continued to reduce its involvement in the conflict. U.S. resolve faded and troop strength diminished. In 1971, the number of troops in Vietnam was reduced to

196,700. February of 1971 was established as a deadline for the removal of another forty-five thousand.

In 1972, North Vietnam launched a massive conventional invasion of South Vietnam that became known as the Easter Offensive. The attacks from the North and from Cambodia threatened to cut South Vietnam in half. President Nixon responded with a massive bombing offensive dubbed Operation Linebacker. Yet the troop withdrawals continued.

On 27 January 1973, the warring parties signed a document in Paris titled, "Ending the War and Restoring Peace in Vietnam." Thus, U.S. involvement in Vietnam ended.

10 THERE'S A WALL IN WASHINGTON

On 13 November 1982, thousands of Vietnam War Veterans marched, not in protest, but rather in support. Their destination was Washington D.C. and the newly constructed Vietnam Veterans Memorial.

"The Wall"—as the memorial has become known—consists of one-hundred forty-four panels forming the now famous "V" shape. The panels of the wall are made of black gabbo stone quarried in Bangalore, India. Bangalore gabbo is world renowned for its highly reflective quality. The Wall is actually two walls that connect at an angle of about 125° at the apex. From the 10.1 foot high apex, the two walls descend in opposite directions down to eight inches on each end. The walls are designated East and West, and each wall contains seventy-two panels. The names of the fallen are etched in chronological order of date of death, beginning at the apex of the East Wall and continuing down to the 70th panel.

The two lowest panels of each wall are blank. The chronology picks up again at the apex of the West Wall descending down to its 70th panel.

Bangalore Gabbo was chosen for the wall because of its highly reflective quality

www.roy-mark.com/Pics_Fixin/Vietnam_Memorial-Flag.jpg

On the West Wall's twelfth panel from the apex, inscribed into the gabbo stone in Optima typeface, are the names James F Lee, Ronald N Parsons, and Richard F Heath.

Ascending to the Wall's thirteenth panel from the apex, is the name William Lorimer IV.

Further up toward the apex on panel ten, the names Arnold L Robbins, John R Stinn, and Melvin R Thomas appear. Inscribed on the ninth panel from the apex are the names Vernon G Bergquist, James G Bulloch, John A Dossett Jr, Franklin D Meyer, Raymond R Uhl, Alonzo H Taylor, and Leslie M Tatarski. On the seventh panel of the West Wall, appear the names Robert E Bauer, Donald A Hall, Jr., Mark R Holtom, Ernest H Laidler, Warren S Lawson, Robert A Painter, Francis J Sullivan, and Douglas M Woodland.

Around the country, other memorials to Vietnam Veterans began to appear. The citizens of Minnesota dedicated the Minnesota Vietnam Veterans Memorial[37] in St. Paul on 26 September 1992. The memorial honors the 1,077 Minnesotans killed and the 43 missing in action in Vietnam. Within the memorial's main plaza, the names of Minnesota's fallen and missing are engraved into a dark green granite wall. Among those many names, one holds special significance to Charlie Company's vets. Engraved in the green granite wall is the name of one of their commanding officers, Captain William Lorimer, IV.

---

[37] www.mvvm.org/imvmd.htm

The Texas Capitol Vietnam Veterans Monument[38] honors all the men and women of Texas who served in the U.S. Armed Forces during the Vietnam War. Entombed inside the monument are personalized dog tags honoring Texans who died or are unaccounted for in Vietnam. One of those dog tags honors Richard Farley Heath of Goldthwaite, Texas. SP6 Heath was killed in the rocket attack on the 229th Assault Helicopter Battalion base at Tay Ninh on 13 April 1970.

Another of the rocket attack victims was Staff Sergeant James Lee. The Lower Alabama Vietnam Veterans Memorial[39], located in Mobile, Alabama, honors each of the 1,213 Alabamans lost in the Vietnam War. Engraved on a wall within the memorial is the name James Franklin Lee.

The Ohio Vietnam Veterans' Memorial[40] is located in Clinton, Ohio. The centerpiece of the memorial is the polished black granite wall made of fifty panels. The wall's gabbo granite was taken from the same quarry in Gabbo, India, as The Vietnam Veterans Memorial Wall in Washington D.C. Engraved below the words "LEST WE FORGET," is the name of C/229th third rocket attack victim, Ronald Neal Parsons.

About a month after Captain Lorimer's arrival at Tay Ninh, PFC John Stinn—barely twenty years old at the time—reported for duty and was assigned work as a clerk in the company orderly room. As such, he and Captain Lorimer, who was the company XO at the time,

---

[38] tcvvm.org
[39] http://alabamavva.org/alamem.html
[40] http://www.ovmp.org/wall.htm

worked in close quarters. Sixty-six days after his CO's tragic death, SP4 Stinn volunteered to man a Huey as a door-gunner. Like his commander, Stinn's name was destined to appear on a memorial in his home state. On Memorial Day of 1984, the State of Iowa dedicated The Iowa Vietnam War Monument[41] on the capital complex in Des Moines. Among the names inscribed on a curved wall is John Richard Stinn.

Two soldiers from 8th Engineer Battalion died when that rocket hit John Stinn's Huey. Like Stinn, Sergeant Melvin Thomas was twenty years old and a Mid-Westerner. On 15 July 1990, the Michigan Vietnam Memorial[42] was officially dedicated at Island Park in Mount Pleasant. On a series of brick monuments are plaques bearing the names of Michigan's service members killed in action. Among the Michiganders memorialized is Melvin Ray Thomas.

The other 8th Engineer Battalion soldier killed along with Stinn and Thomas was Staff Sergeant Arnold Robbins. In July of 1984, the Buffalo Arts Commission dedicated a memorial to Western New York's Vietnam Veterans. The Western New York Vietnam Veterans Memorial consists of two quarter-circular granite walls rising about twelve feet from the ground with a granite column centered between the two walls. Engraved upon the column, below the words, "Western New York Vietnam Veterans," is the image of a soldier and a helicopter. Upon the two walls are engraved the names of Western New Yorkers that made the ultimate sacrifice

---

[41] http://iowapowmia.us/?q=node/105
[42] www.vietmemorialmi.com/

in Vietnam. One of the names engraved upon the wall is that of Arnold Lee Robbins.

Twenty-seven days after the loss of John Stinn and the two 8th Engineer Battalion sergeants, Charlie Company suffered the loss of all onboard Huey 66-16985 when it crashed in a severe thunderstorm in Tay Ninh Provence. The names of all five killed in that nighttime tragedy appear together on the Vietnam Veterans Memorial in Washington D.C. SP4 Raymond Uhl, 9-8-5's crew chief, sitting in the co-pilot's seat on that doomed flight, is memorialized by his home state. The Colorado Freedom Memorial[43] was dedicated on Memorial Day 2013. The memorial is located in Aurora, Colorado, on a four-acre parcel near Buckley Air Force Base. The memorial is made of glass, stands 12 feet tall, and is 95 feet long. The glass panels that make up the memorial reflect Colorado's mountains and blue skies; the panels lean forward and back to represent men falling in action. Etched on the glass panels are the names of nearly six-thousand Coloradans killed or missing in action from all of America's wars. On panel 18, Column 3, Row 49 is the name Raymond Riede Uhl.

The door-gunner on the night Huey 66-16985 crashed was SP4 Alonzo Taylor. On 10 December 1988, Taylor's home state of California dedicated The California Vietnam Veterans Memorial[44]. The memorial sits at the northeast corner of State Capitol Park in Sacramento. Twenty engraved black granite panels stand within the

---

[43] www.cfmf.net/
[44] http://capitolmuseum.ca.gov/
VirtualTour.aspx?Content1=1416&Content2=1428&Content3=1302

circular memorial. Engraved on the panels are the names of at least 5,800 of California's dead or missing, along with their hometowns. Among the engravings is the name of Alonzo Hughes Taylor of Pomona, California.

The doomed Huey flew into the nighttime thunderstorm with one Charlie Company and two Alpha Company passengers sitting in the back of 9-8-5. Alpha Company's SP4 John Dossett was from Lamar, Missouri. The state of Missouri does not have a statewide memorial, but John is not forgotten by his high school in Lamar. On crisp fall Friday nights, football fans gather to support their Lamar High School Tigers. Before each game, football fans stand and face Old Glory at the south end of the field. As they sing the National Anthem, the Stars and Stripes waves over a small memorial to the school's Vietnam War dead. Engraved on the memorial, in chronological order of date of death, are the names of six Lamar High School alumni that sacrificed their lives. The last inscription reads, "Sgt. John A Dossett Jr - Killed in Action - June 11, 1970."[45]

The other Alpha Company passenger riding with Dossett in the back of 9-8-5 was SP4 Vernon Bergquist. From Spencer, Iowa, Bergquist is memorialized on The Iowa Vietnam War Monument[46] on the capital complex in Des Moines. Bergquist and John Stinn served in different 229th companies at Tay Ninh; in life, they likely didn't know each other or realized that their hometowns were about one-hundred miles apart. In death, their

---

[45] SP4 John Dossett, Jr. was posthumously promoted to Sergeant E-5.
[46] http://iowapowmia.us/?q=node/105

names are inscribed nearby on a curved wall on The Iowa Vietnam War Monument.

Charlie Company's passenger on 9-8-5 on the fateful night of the crash was SP4 Franklin Meyer. Meyer's home of record was the small community of Smicksburg, about seventy miles northeast of Pittsburg. The largest Vietnam memorial in Pennsylvania is in Pittsburg, but it honors only fallen Vietnam Veterans from the Pittsburg area. Franklin Delano Meyer's name does not appear on a memorial within the state of Pennsylvania.

The aircraft commander of Huey 66-16985 when it crashed into the rice paddy on the night of 11 June 1970 was WO1 James Bulloch. Bulloch was posthumously promoted to chief warrant officer (W2), but as of this writing, James Grady Bulloch's name does not appear on a memorial within his home state of New Mexico. There is a Vietnam Memorial[47] in Angle Fire, New Mexico, but the names of that state's war dead are not engraved upon a single monument. Within the memorial complex, an Army UH-1D Huey Helicopter—Tail Number 64-13670—stands guard over the park and a Veterans Memorial Walkway. The walkway is lined with bricks commemorating all United States veterans. Bricks commemorating individual veterans may be purchased and are laid alongside the walkway once each year.

WO1 Les "Tango" Tatarski has been memorialized in his home state of New York. Fourteen years after that "hover-down and kick-out" mission inside Cambodia, the Western New York Vietnam Veterans Memorial in

---

[47] www.vietnamveteransmemorial.org

Buffalo inscribed his name on one of the two granite columns within the memorial. Near the image of a helicopter is the name Leslie Miles Tatarski.

September 26th, 1970, is etched in the memories of North Flaggers who were in Vietnam at the time as the single worst day in the Company's proud history. Eight of their own were killed in a single event that resonates in their memories and nightmares to this day. In Vietnam, they were all brothers in arms, all Charlie Company North Flaggers; back in the world, they were New Englanders, Mid-Westerners, Southerners, and Westerners. They are remembered and memorialized.

The Kansas Vietnam Veterans Memorial[48] was erected in Junction City and dedicated on 4 July 1987. On four of seven black granite panels standing thirteen feet tall are inscribed the names of 753 Kansans killed in Vietnam. One of the names is Cherry Buster's last aircraft commander, WO1 Mark Richard Holtom.

In California, an Army Huey stands vigil over the names of Long Beach sons killed in the Vietnam War. Appropriately, the Huey, too, is a Vietnam Vet, having logged over two thousand combat hours in Vietnam. The Long Beach Vietnam Veterans Memorial[49] was dedicated on Veterans Day, 11 November 2000. Mark Richard Holtom's official home of record was Baldwin, Kansas, but he had grown up in and around Long Beach. His name, along with Long Beach's other fallen sons was inscribed on a bronze plaque at the base of the Huey. In 2013, a family member of one those heroes brought her

[48] www.junctioncity.org/index.aspx?nid=145
[49] www.vietvet.org/longbeach.htm

young son to the memorial to pay respects to the memory of a relative he never knew. As they approached the Huey, she was shocked to see a park-worker removing the bronze plaque. When asked why he was removing the plaque, the worker explained that it had been replaced several times after thieves had removed it surreptitiously, the bronze to be converted to cash to feed drug habits. Drug addicts, it seems, respect no moral boundaries in their quest to feed their habits. The bronze plaque on the Long Beach Memorial was replaced with one of plastic. The plastic plaque now pays grim tribute to the fallen heroes and is a reminder of the society they could not have imagined.

Sitting in Cherry Buster's co-pilot seat on 26 September 1970 was First Lieutenant Francis Sullivan. A memorial in his home state of Connecticut was erected and dedicated in Coventry on 17 May 2008. The Connecticut Vietnam Veterans Memorial[50] was inspired by a book simply titled *612*. The book was the result of a 2001 project by schoolchildren of Captain Nathan Hale Middle School in Coventry. Their teacher, Thomas Dzicek, had challenged his students to identify and learn more about each of Connecticut's servicemen who died in the Vietnam War. The fruits of those middle-schoolers spawned the inspiration of Jean Risley to erect a Vietnam memorial in Connecticut. The memorial would honor the Connecticutians that made the ultimate sacrifice. Engraved on black granite quarried in South

---

[50] www.cvvm.org/

Africa are the names of each of Connecticut's 612 fallen soldiers, airmen, sailors, and marines.

Lieutenant Sullivan was posthumously promoted; the name of Captain Francis Jordan Sullivan is inscribed, along with the others on the monument, below the words "ALL GAVE SOME - SOME GAVE ALL."

SP4 Donald "Spoon" Hall, Charlie Company's cook turned crew chief was in his position behind his aircraft commander when Cherry Buster collided with Thumpy 1. Almost twenty years later, Hall's name was inscribed on a memorial in his home state. On 15 July 1990, the Michigan Vietnam Memorial[51] was officially dedicated at Island Park in Mount Pleasant. On a series of brick monuments are plaques bearing the names of Michigan's service members killed in action, including Donald Allen Hall, Jr. SP4 Donald Hall was posthumously promoted to sergeant E-5.

Sitting in Cherry Buster's door-gunner's position was SP4 Ernest Laidler. The twenty-year-old had served just thirty-one days in Vietnam when the mid-air collision took his life. Laidler's home state of Massachusetts honors his service with the Massachusetts Vietnam Veterans Memorial[52] in Worcester. The memorial is on a four-acre site in Green Hill Park and was dedicated on 9 June 2002. Engraved on stone pillars within the memorial complex are the names of 1,546 Massachusetts sons and one daughter killed or missing in Vietnam. On one of the pillars is engraved the name Ernest Hammond Laidler.

---

[51] www.vietmemorialmi.com/
[52] www.massvvm.org/

Huey 68-16123, a.k.a. Thumpy 1, was in the lead position when it was hit from behind by Cherry Buster. Thumpy 1's co-pilot that day was First Lieutenant Warren Lawson. In the Florida Panhandle city of Pensacola, a one-half scale replica of the Vietnam Veterans Memorial in Washington, D.C. was erected. Dedicated on 24 October 1992, the Vietnam Veterans Wall South[53] is enclosed within a five-and-one-half-acre site overlooking Pensacola Bay. Guarding over The Wall South is a UH-1 Huey, on loan from the National Museum of Naval Aviation in Pensacola. Inscribed on Panel W7, Line 93 is the name Warren Stephen Lawson, a Floridian whose home in Milton, Florida, was just twenty-seven miles away. As in Washington, the names of the fallen are inscribed in chronological order of date of death; and as in Washington, the crews of Cherry Buster and Thumpy 1 are together on the wall as they died in Vietnam. Appropriately, engraved at the base of the park's flagpole are the words, "TOGETHER THEN, TOGETHER AGAIN."

In 1986, a memorial was constructed behind the Arizona State Capitol Complex. The names of Arizonans killed in the Vietnam War, including that of Thumpy 1's crew chief, Douglas Woodland, posthumously promoted to sergeant E-5. Engraved into one of the ten black marble pillars of the memorial is the name Douglas Mead Woodland.

Thumpy 1's door-gunner, SP4 Robert Painter, was one of 1,046 Marylanders killed during the Vietnam War. On

---

[53] www.pensacolawallsouth.org/home.html

28 May 1989, the Maryland Vietnam Veterans Memorial[54] was dedicated on a three-and-a-half-acre site within Baltimore's Middle Branch Park. The Memorial consists of a ring of stones and a granite wall upon which the name Robert Albert Painter, Jr. is inscribed.

WO1 Bob "Little Ogre" Bauer was leading the flight of four Hueys on the morning of 26 September 1970. Four-thousand feet above a small, deserted Vietnamese village, called Rang Rang, the twenty-three-year-old New York native keyed his mike for the last time. His last message was a testament to his bravery and character. The airways crackled with, "Goood Morning Vietnam... We've just had a mid-air collision." Some communities in the State of New York have built memorials to Vietnam Veterans. There currently is not, however, a memorial dedicated to all New Yorkers who died in Vietnam. Although the name Robert Ernest Bauer is inscribed on The Wall in Washington, D.C., it does not appear on any memorial within his home state.

---

[54] www.mdva.state.md.us/MMMC/vietnamVetsMemorial.html

11 SPIRIT IN THE SKY

Flying out of Vietnam and back to the world is a flight no Vietnam Veteran will ever forget. Sadly, over fifty-eight thousand of America's finest did not live to see that day. Some were "New Guys," having arrived in-country just days before they died. Some were short-timers; a few days more—and a wake-up—and they would have caught a "freedom bird" back to the world for a reunion with their families.

According to the National Archives[55], 58,220 Americans were killed in Vietnam and Cambodia. Of that number, about 18% died not by the enemy's hand, but rather by unfortunate accidents. Not surprisingly, the percentage of deaths resulting from helicopter accidents is greater than the average. In this book, we have learned of the deaths of nineteen helicopter pilots, crewmembers, and passengers. Fourteen of those deaths, some 74%, were the result of two accidents. The nighttime crash of UH-1H 66-16985 in a thunderstorm on 11 June 1970 took the lives of five good men. Eight men were lost in the mid-air collision of

---

[55] National Archives Document: Statistical Information about Fatal Casualties of the Vietnam War (www.archives.gov/research/military/vietnam-war/casualty-statistics.html)

26 September 1970.

Sadly, the final flight for Charlie Company's Vietnam War dead was in flag-draped aluminum boxes. Symbolically, however, they are on a final flight to the heavens.

On 7 February 1999, NASA launched STARDUST on a mission to collect samples of a comet and return them to Earth. Onboard the spacecraft, etched on four microchips were over one million names, including the names of the 58,220 Americans that died during the Vietnam War. One set of microchips returned to earth when the Stardust samples returned in 2006. Onboard Stardust, etched on identical microchips, are the names:

Robert Ernest Bauer
Vernon Gail Bergquist
James Grady Bulloch
John Adrian Dossett, Jr.
Donald Allen Hall, Jr.
Richard Farley Heath
Mark Richard Holtom
Ernest Hammond Laidler
Warren Stephen Lawson
James Franklin Lee
William Lorimer, IV

Franklin Delano Meyer
Robert Albert Painter, Jr.
Ronald Neal Parsons
Arnold Lee Robbins
John Richard Stinn
Francis Jordan Sullivan
Leslie Miles Tatarski
Alonzo Hughes Taylor
Melvin Ray Thomas
Raymond Riede Uhl
Douglas Mead Woodland

Their names remain in space to this day in an eternal circumnavigation of our sun. They will be remembered.

These men suffered all
Sacrificed all
Dared all-and died

INTERNET PHOTOS

A Note From the Author

Over the course of my research into the events of which you have just read, I contacted, and was contacted by many 229th Assault Helicopter Battalion veterans. In addition to sharing their memories, they also shared many of their old Vietnam photos, some of which appear in this book. All of the photos that appear in this book, plus many more are available for viewing on my website. Although many of the original photos are in color, they appear in this book—by necessity—in black and white.

The quality of the photos on my website is better than was possible in this book, and the color photographs appear in color.

www.roymark.org/fixin-to-die-rag-photos.html

—Roy Mark

APPENDIX

Charlie Company, 229th Assault Helicopter Battalion K.I.A

The list is arranged chronologically according to date of death from 1966 to 1970.

The Wall Location Column gives the panel number and location (East or West Wall) and the Line Number on the Vietnam Veterans Memorial in Washington, D.C.

Name	Pay Grade	Date of Death	Home of Record	Wall Location	Age
Jefferson, Herman Louis Jr.	E-4	12 Nov 1965	New Orleans, LA	3E L44	32
Zamora, Carlos Jr.	E-5	28 Jan 1966	Carrizozo, NM	4E L105	21
Estes, Donald Cathell	W-2	24 Jun 1966	Auburn, AL	8E L84	30
Leburm, Lawrence P	E-3	24 Jun 1966	Philadelphia, PA	8E L87	19
Steier, William Edward	E-3	24 Jun 1966	Binghamton, NY	8E L89	22
Woods, Lawrence Dane	O-3	24 Jun 1966	Hartford, CT	8E L90	29

ROY MARK

Name	Pay Grade	Date of Death	Home of Record	Wall Location	Age
McLeary, Orval Wade	W-1	6 May 1968	Sturdivant, MO	56E L13	31
Han, Charles William	E-4	20 Nov 1968	Inverness, MT	W38 L17	22
Clime, Ralph John	W-1	19 Jun 1969	Marcellus, MI	W22 L86	21
Matthews, Henry Don	E-4[56]	19 Jun 1969	Rogers, AR	W22 L91	21
Pearlstein, Jerrold Sherman	W-1	19 Jun 1969	Los Angeles, CA	W22 L92	20
Voss, Raymond Allen	E-4[57]	19 Jun 1969	Seattle, WA	W22 L94	20
Havel, Michael Dennis	E-5	26 Jun 1969	Reading, MA	W21 L18	22
Allmers, Robert Roger	E-4	10 Dec 1969	Oshkosh, WI	W15 L45	22
Swayze, Gerald Clifford	O-3	30 Dec 1969	Wilmot, SD	W15 L112	28
Lorimer, William IV	O-3	10 Mar 1970	St. Cloud, MN	W13 L105	27
Lee, James Franklin	E-6	3 Apr 1970	Gallion, AL	W12 L89	26

[56] Henry Matthews was posthumously promoted to Sergeant E-5
[57] Raymond Voss was posthumously promoted to Sergeant E-5

Name	Pay Grade	Date of Death	Home of Record	Wall Location	Age
Parsons, Ronald Neal	E-4	3 Apr 1970	Wapakoneta, OH	W12 L89	21
Heath, Richard Farley	E-6	13 Apr 1970	Goldthwaite, TX	W12 L132	22
Stinn, John Richard	E-4	15 Apr 1970	Panama, IA	W10 L47	20
Bulloch, James Grady	W-1[58]	11 Jun 1970	Albuquerque, NM	W9 L42	32
Taylor, Alonzo Hughes	E-4	11 Jun 1970	Pomona, CA	W9 L45	21
Uhl, Raymond Riede	E-4[59]	11 Jun 1970	Denver, CO	W9 L44	21
Tatarski, Leslie Miles	W-1	12 Jun 1970	Buffalo, NY	W9 L49	21
Bauer, Robert Ernest	W-1	26 Sept 1970	Pearl River, NY	W7 L91	23
Hall, Donald Allen Jr.	E-4[60]	26 Sept 1970	Millington, MI	W7 L92	21
Holtom, Mark Richard	W-1	26 Sept 1970	Baldwin City, KS	W7 L93	21

[58] James G. Bulloch was posthumously promoted to chief warrant officer W-2
[59] Raymond Riede Uhl was posthumously promoted to Sergeant E-5
[60] Donald Allen Hall, Jr. was posthumously promoted to Sergeant E-5

Name	Pay Grade	Date of Death	Home of Record	Wall Location	Age
Laidler, Ernest Hammond	E-4	26 Sept 1970	Abington, MA	W7 L93	20
Lawson, Warren Stephen	O-2	26 Sept 1970	Milton, FL	W7 L93	22
Painter, Robert Allen	E-4	26 Sept 1970	Indian Head, MD	W7 L94	20
Sullivan, Francis Jordan	O-2[61]	26 Sept 1970	East Hartford, CT	W7 L94	27
Woodland, Douglas Mead	E-4[62]	26 Sept 1970	Scottsdale, AZ	W7 L95	19

---

[61] Francis Sullivan was posthumously promoted to Captain O-3
[62] Douglas Woodland was posthumously promoted to Sergeant E-5

INDEX

ABOUT THE AUTHOR

Roy Mark grew up in New Orleans. He joined the U.S. Marine Corps in 1963 and received his basic training at Parris Island, South Carolina. He later served as a radiotelegraph operator with the First Anti-Tank Battalion at Camp Pendleton and with the Marine Communications Detachment onboard the USS Mount McKinley (AGC-7). His final assignment was as an instructor at the Radiotelegraph School, Marine Corps Recruit Depot, San Diego. During his service, he served nine days in Vietnam in support of Vietnamese Counteroffensive (Phase II) during July of 1966.

Mr. Mark attended Southeastern Louisiana University before beginning a career in the oil industry. In a career spanning three decades, he worked as a mud engineer, mud school instructor, oil well blowout prevention instructor, and drilling supervisor.

Roy has worked in locations around the world, including North and South America, Europe, and Southeast Asia. He lived in Indonesia from 1988 until relocating to Chiang Mai, Thailand in 2001.

Mr. Mark has written technical manuals on oil well blowout prevention for two companies and has written numerous short stories. He published "The Mark Family History" in 2005 and "The Texan and The Ice-Boy" in 2014.

Please visit Roy Mark's social media sites:

RoyMark.Org   Facebook.com/Roy.Mark.Books

24757958R00101